News

News

THE POLITICS OF ILLUSION

W. Lance Bennett
University of Washington

Longman
New York & London

News
The Politics of Illusion

Longman Inc., 1560 Broadway, New York, N.Y. 10036
Associated companies, branches, and representatives
throughout the world.

Developmental Editor: Irving E. Rockwood
Editorial and Design Supervisor: Diane Perlmuth
Production Supervisor: Ferne Y. Kawahara
Manufacturing Supervisor: Marion Hess

Library of Congress Cataloging in Publication Data

Bennett, W. Lance.
  News, the politics of illusion.

  Includes index.
  1. Journalism—Political aspects—United States.
I. Title.
PN4888.P6B46 1983   070.4'3   82-22851
ISBN 0-582-28335-3 (pbk.)

Printing: 9 8 7 6 5 4 3 2   Year: 91 90 89 88 87 86 85
Manufactured in the United States of America

Contents

Acknowledgments

I am indebted to a number of people for helping me to think more clearly about the political implications of the news. Due to their patience and generosity, the time spent writing this book has been both personally enjoyable and intellectually satisfying. First, a word of thanks goes to my colleagues at the University of Washington who endured all those fuzzy discussions about what I thought I was trying to do. I am particularly grateful to Bill Haltom, Jude Tomamichel, Dan Lev, Stu Scheingold, Alex Edelstein, David Olson, Don McCrone, Liz McHale, Paul Peretz, Jonathan Pool, and Don Matthews. An award for showing me how to spend hours in front of the television without going crazy goes to Martha Feldman, who does the best instant news analysis of anyone I know. I am also indebted to Kathleen Hance for bringing me back to earth on a regular basis by asking me persistently that dreaded question: "What are you trying to say?" Don Morrissey helped me answer that question during our Thursday night explorations of life and politics. Murray Edelman has been a continuing source of inspiration for my thinking about politics. I am indebted to his wise comments on the parts of the argument that I presented to his NEH summer seminar at the University of Wisconsin. Lloyd Bitzer also made the stop in Madison a rewarding experience. The Department of Rhetoric and Communication and the Department of Political Science at SUNY Albany provided another valuable opportunity to take this show on the road before its official debut. A sabbatical year granted by the University of Washington made the research and writing a real pleasure. The unsung secretarial heroics of Sharon Clark, Mary Pierce, and Brahmi Warich turned my questionable longhand into a thing of typographical beauty.

Working with the people at Longman has been a joy. Irv Rockwood not only read the drafts but knew precisely what to say and how to say it (the Editor of the Year Award to Irv). Jerry Manheim proved to be the perfect critic. His comments almost always hit the mark, and his enthusiasm for the project made the revision process almost tolerable.

Finally, a special thanks goes to Miss Nancy Ann Searcy, my third-grade teacher. She first introduced me to the world of news with a subscription to *My Weekly Reader*. The world seems much different to me now than it did then, but somehow the news remains much the same.

INTRODUCTION

The News Puzzle

> I really look with commiseration over the
> great body of my fellow citizens who,
> reading newspapers, live and die in the
> belief that they have known something
> of what has been passing in the world
> in their time.
>
> HARRY TRUMAN

We can only imagine what Harry Truman might have said about the fates
of modern Americans who live in a news world dominated by television,
not newspapers—Americans who are exposed to ever simpler images of
an ever more complex world, Americans who are the targets of increasingly sophisticated communication techniques designed to control
the balance of power on the important issues affecting their lives. It is
little wonder that the news is one of the most controversial subjects of our
times. Mentioning the news is likely to trigger strong views on matters
such as the political biases of reporters, the latest threat to the freedom of
the press, or whether anyone will ever really replace Walter Cronkite.

Despite the multitude of positions taken by journalists, scholars, politicians, and the public, the news remains a puzzle. On the one hand, few
things are as much a part of our lives as the news. With the advent of
sophisticated mass communication, the news has become a sort of instant
historical record of the pace, progress, problems, and hopes of society.
On the other hand—and here's the puzzle—the news provides, at best, a
superficial and distorted image of society. Although American life is satu-
rated with information, the typical news fare covers only a narrow range
of issues, from the viewpoints of an even narrower range of sources, with
emphases placed on drama over depth, human interest over social significance, and formula reporting over perceptive analysis. The puzzle, put
simply, is this: How can anything so superficial be so central to our lives?

The search for an answer to this question takes us on a behind-the-
scenes tour of American politics and mass communication. This explora-
tion reveals that the three major actors in the news process—politicians,
journalists, and the public—occupy quite different positions in both the

political structure and the mass communication system. Despite the vast differences in the three political worlds, each contains certain conditions that reinforce the same superficial news. This means that problems with the news are not minor, accidental, or temporary departures from American norms about freedom of information in a democracy. Flaws in the news are the results of structural conditions in our political system.

The causes of superficial news are too deeply rooted to respond to the all-too-familiar calls for reforms in areas such as government secrecy, news reporting practices, and citizen education. Their comforting tones and reassuring simplicity notwithstanding, these reform proposals have not worked. They have not worked for a simple reason: They cannot work. Most of the reforms suggested by even the harshest critics of government-press relations are based on romantic notions about untapped cadres of public-minded politicians, future legions of journalist-heroes who will be immune to the profit motives of their news organizations, and a growing mass of aroused citizens who will wield decision-making power if only they have a little more information about what they are deciding. These hopes for change, appealing as they are, simply do not square with political reality in America.

Consider, briefly, the "news politics" of politicians, journalists, and the public. From the standpoint of politicians, it has always been clear that power and influence in a democratic society depend on the control and strategic use of information. The battle for information traditionally has been intense among interest groups, government, and the public. However, the public is increasingly losing ground to public officials and economic interests who have helped perpetuate the belief that major policy areas of government, like economic planning and national security, are well beyond the knowledge and judgment of the average citizen. The fact that these issues also seem to be beyond the knowledge and judgment of average politicians and bureaucrats does not alter the remarkably low levels of accountability surrounding their decisions. As long as information control is essential to the accumulation of power, and as long as information control is tacitly justified by fears of an informed public, political actors will never be compelled to release candid news of their political dealings.

The politics of information, power, and decision making also carry gloomy prospects for journalistic reforms. As long as the distribution of power is narrow and decision processes are closed, journalists will never be free of their dependence on the small group of public relations experts, official spokespersons, and powerful leaders whose self-serving pronouncements have become firmly established as the bulk of the daily news.

The prospects for an enlightened citizenry are not much brighter than the hopes for noble politicians or crusading journalists. As long as the public has little political access and even less power, there will be little substance behind the familiar democratic rhetoric that somehow equates all decisions of state with the public interest. Even though the masses of people never participate directly in the actual decisions that affect their lives, they receive through the news the constant impression that American democracy, despite its flaws, still works better than any other brand. The "advertisements for authority" that dominate the news are surrounded by other reports that convey fearful images of violent crime, economic insecurity, and nuclear war. Such images reinforce public support for political authorities who promise order, security, and responsive political solutions. In short, the news provides little stimulus for enlightenment and few opportunities for expression should people attain their enlightenment elsewhere. In fact, the routine nature of news would seem to work against the elevation of civic consciousness by providing people with easy psychological escapes from the unpleasant reality of powerlessness.

The above ideas and others to be developed in these pages are not easy for many Americans to think about, much less to accept. Before most of us were able to think or reason for ourselves, we were taught to believe that America is the world's greatest democracy and that freedom of the press is one of its main foundations. This dominant socialization makes it hard to see either the power gap between authorities and the public, or the degree of information control that traps the news-hungry press.

When faced with a choice between confronting an unpleasant reality and defending a set of comforting and socially accepted beliefs, most people choose the latter course. For example, it is common to hear people defend the news as an accurate and useful reflection of society and politics (never mind its domination by the "news factories" of government, business, and interest groups). It is also easy to rationalize the flaws in the news merely by affirming that, whatever its problems, it is still better than in Russia. (This is true, but what is gained from comparing something to the worst imaginable case?) Some people make excuses by condemning the superficiality of mass news sources like television, but noting the existence of excellent journals and magazines for those who care to take their news seriously. (What credibility do such "highbrow," low-readership sources have when pitted against the mainstream news corps of respected journalists who represent the latest official pronouncements as objective news for the masses?) Other people even take the offensive and criticize the news as too antiauthority due to the left-wing bias of journalists. (Leaving aside the obvious news production edge held by the government and influential "right-wing" actors, just how much subversion really lives in the hearts of reporters who are, at worst, professional, upper-middle-class, civic-minded, liberal Democrats?) It is true that some people do condemn news superficiality as a serious and unqualified problem, but their overwhelming response is to call for the sorts of naive reforms, mentioned earlier, that reflect more a faith in democratic myths than an understanding of political realities.

Perhaps the most significant response to news is the one that is missing: the virtual absence of credible public figures pointing out the flaws in the news and explaining those flaws in terms of the realities of power and information in American politics. Since the news is a major source of what people regard as true, objective, and real in the world around them, it would not serve the separate purposes of politicians, press, or public to accept news that undermines itself. However, it is not very comforting to know that people pay such a high price for the comforts of an "objective reality" that is the illusory product of a vicious cycle of news and politics. In this cycle, "official" versions of reality are legitimized because they dominate news content, and the news, in turn, seems "objective" because official versions of events fall into such familiar, standardized patterns.

The first step toward understanding this news politics problem is to gain an appreciation of how serious a problem it really is. Chapter 1 is devoted to understanding superficial news and its political effects. Following this overview of the problem, the core of the book looks at the three sets of actors responsible for news politics. Chapter 2 shows how powerful political actors attempt to control news content. Chapter 3 explains how journalists unwittingly promote the propaganda of those political actors. Chapter 4 addresses the question of why the American people remain attentive to the illusory, but dramatic, political images contained in the news. Based on this analysis of how the news is produced, communicated, and consumed, the concluding chapter explores the problem of why the news persists in its present form, and shows how the concerned citizen can make better use of the information provided by the mass media.

A Note to the Reader

- Why is a society that is so rich in information populated with people who are so confused about politics?
- Is it possible for journalism to be objective as it is practiced in America?
- Is the news mainly an "advertisement for the system," or is it a valuable citizen resource?

These are just a few of the questions you will encounter in this book. In the final analysis, it is up to you to draw conclusions about them. In order to stimulate your thinking, the book presents a perspective that is critical of the news—a perspective intended to provoke thought and reaction. I have chosen to present a broad, alternative point of view for a simple reason: There would be little gained by going over the story of the free press in America for yet another time. As an American citizen you already know by heart the saga of "A Free Press and A Free People." True, you may have forgotten a few characters or some of the episodes. Nevertheless, memorizing those missing facts once again would not change the plot about how the enduring struggle for freedom of speech and information has created the foundation for democracy in America. Since you know this story already, you should use it in thinking about the arguments in this book. Don't feel that you must accept either the story of the free press or the perspective in this book in its entirety. Use the two perspectives to challenge one another and to draw your own conclusions. After all, the capacity to think independently, without fear or insecurity, is the foundation on which our political freedom rests.

ONE

Mass Media News

"Eyewitless" news contains little in the way of useful information ... of ongoing, integrated issues and concerns, of attempts to dig beneath the surface for more enduring truths and subtle shadings—a twinkie of the airwaves.

RON POWERS

Americans live in a vast information and communication empire. The number of media outlets is staggering. By the latest count, there are some 1700 daily newspapers in the United States, with a combined circulation of more than 60 million. There are also more than 7000 weekly papers and countless periodicals aimed at audiences like college students, ethnic groups, religious sects, foreign-language speakers, and business and professional groups. The broadcast media are equally prolific, with nearly 4500 AM radio channels, some 3000 commercial FM stations, over 1100 educational FM bands, 750 commercial television stations, and nearly 400 educational TV channels.[1] The national addiction to mass media is perhaps best captured by the fact that more American homes have television sets than flush toilets.

The abundance of such information sources would seem to lend credence to the old adage that there is no excuse for people to be uninformed about the world in which they live. It is, after all, tempting to conclude that if members of a "mass mediated" society like ours are ignorant of politics and world affairs, then they simply have not bothered to become informed. Yet many people are not informed. Opinion research indicates that many citizens—perhaps the majority—live in a state of confusion and ignorance about government and political issues. What are we to make of this paradox that one of the most sophisticated communication societies in the world is populated by poorly informed individuals?

Before leaping to the conclusion that the fault resides with apathetic citizens, consider the possibility that the problem lies primarily with the nature of the news itself. Despite the common assumption that profes-

1

sional news organizations provide clear, informative, and fairly objective pictures of the world, there is a growing body of evidence to the contrary. Recent research is beginning to paint a portrait of the news as fragmented, analytically superficial, hard to remember, and difficult to use meaningfully. Only rarely does the news contain solid explanations, and even less often does it present clear conclusions about events. It is also becoming apparent that the media are far from "objective" in their coverage. We shall see, for example, that the views of powerful political and economic actors dominate the news, while the concerns of groups outside the mainstream are typically ignored or presented in negative ways.

In view of these and other problems with the news, the citizen's best efforts to become informed may be counterproductive: the more news consumed, the more narrow and stereotypical the resulting understandings may become. But how can such a situation exist when there are so many free and competitive information channels in the United States? In order to answer this important question, we must first distinguish mass media channels from more restricted information sources and then separate the quantity of information from its quality.

First, it must be acknowledged that there are hundreds, if not thousands, of small publications, listener-sponsored radio and television stations, and public access cable channels that offer a broad range of clear and detailed perspectives on public affairs. However, for reasons that will be discussed later, news sources that exist outside mass media are not credible in the eyes of most Americans. Diverse viewpoints matter little if they are not taken seriously. We are, like it or not, prisoners of mass media. Therefore, it is the nature of mass media news that we must understand.

Even if the mass media dictate the terms of accepted political reality in America, it would seem that there are so many respected media outlets transmitting so much sheer information that the concerned citizen should be able to assemble an accurate and sophisticated view of the world. It is true that media organizations differ considerably in terms of the quantity of information they transmit and the range of topics they cover. Nevertheless, underneath these differences in information quantity and subject matter lies a common core of remarkably similar political messages.

How can the basic political messages of mass media news be pretty much the same whether we listen to the two minutes of headlines every hour on our favorite radio station or spend the week trying to digest the ten-pound Sunday edition of the *New York Times*? Technical answers to this question will be presented later in this book when we explore the interworkings of journalism and politics. For now, let's start with a simple, common-sense distinction between the form and the substance of news. Much can be learned about a product by distinguishing the packaging from the contents.

In what sense is the news a "product"? It surely differs from corn flakes and underarm deodorants. Yet the news shares one important thing in common with most commercial products: It is marketed effectively through the creation of product images. Such images promote the illusion of distinctiveness while blurring the underlying reality of the product. One brand of corn flakes conveys an image of crunchiness, another exudes healthiness, while still another promises a fantasy of family togetherness at the breakfast table. Similarly, if our desire is to keep in touch with world events, we are invited to do so by becoming an "eyewitness," taking an adventure into the world of "action news," turning ourselves over to a respected "news authority," or sitting down with the serious purpose of reading "All the News That's Fit to Print." While there is no doubt that the consumer of mass media has choices, the important question is whether those choices differ in any meaningful way.

Have you ever wondered why Pontiac, Chevrolet, and Buick sell very similar car models with different names and at different prices? It is, to put it simply, much more profitable to mass produce the same product and sell it in personalized packaging than it is to produce many distinctive products. If the marketing goal is to capture large segments of the mass buying public, it is more efficient to sell everyone pretty much the same thing than to undermine profits by designing something different for everyone. This is where packaging comes in. Packages convey images. They dress products up or down. They give off signals about the social status (real or desired) of the people who use particular products. Packages even fit products into the life styles of consumers—the pace, taste, zest, zip, rush, whoosh (and let's not forget those springtime moments) of life itself.

The news is, above all, a consumer good. It would not exist in the diverse forms that we know it without the marketing strategies that deliver (or, better put, "sell") news audiences to advertisers. In order to sell audiences to sponsors, the news must be "sold" to the audience in the first place. That is, the news product must fit into the audience's social image, life style, and daily schedule. Americans differ greatly in terms of social images, life styles, and daily schedules. It is worth considering that much of what passes for diversity in mass media news is largely a matter of packaging designed to deliver a product to market. Once this packaging is removed, it is possible to see that behind the various forms of news, there is a remarkable uniformity of content.

Form Triumphs over Substance: News Styles and Life Styles

It is hard to imagine anything, short of the air we breathe, that is easier to consume than news. The saturation of everyday life with news is no small feat, considering the diversity of American life styles. Differences in age, wealth, education, occupation, religion, social customs, and leisure pursuits all have effects on the ways in which people receive, interpret, and use news information.[2] Despite such differences in American society, the news reaches most people one way or another. Forms of news are designed to fit most personal schedules. People who drive the freeways to and from work can tune their car radios to morning and evening "drive time" news. People who spend early-morning hours at home can choose among the big budget "news and features" programs produced by the major television networks. Newspapers and magazines reach wide readerships and offer people considerable choice about where and when to read the news. Local evening news programs on television often run for two or three hours in order to accommodate different work and dinner schedules. Any gaps that may exist in this news barrage are filled by other sources like an all-news cable television network; all-news radio stations; regular newscasts scattered throughout radio and television entertainment programming; late-night radio talk shows; and the news-in-review features of weekend radio, television, and newspapers. People who somehow elude this incredible communication net will often make contact with friends or strangers who ask the familiar question, "Did you hear the news about_____?" It is virtually impossible to avoid the news. This is a statement that cannot be made about other foundations of society like religion, organized politics, or work.

Not only is the news available to virtually everyone, but it is delivered in forms that are finely tuned to individual tastes, needs, and self-images. The formats of newspapers span the spectrum of information appetites from the serious to the sensational. Early-morning network television programs offer viewers strikingly different presentations of much the same information. One program invites the audience in for morning coffee with a folksy host—a former television actor—who sits and chats with guests in a living room–like set. Other viewers can watch a serious newscast format anchored by an affable pair of news professionals. The third network presents a cast of bubbly-but-credible personalities who read the news, clown through the weather, and exchange quips on a set that could double for a late-night talk show.

The marked differences in news formats indicate how much a part of everyday life the news has become. People may be exposed to the same disaster stories or the same grim reports on the economy, but it helps to receive the information in ways that minimize the gap between the stark realities of the world and the familiar routines of private lives. Market studies show, for example, that people personalize their relations with a favorite television newscaster. Many people prefer to hear the news from someone they identify as a concerned friend, an image that made former

CBS newscaster Walter Cronkite the most preferred news source in America. In fact, when Cronkite retired, CBS fell from first to last place in the network nightly news ratings. The dramatic drop in audience share was attributed to the fact that fewer people were attracted to Cronkite's replacement, Dan Rather, who projected a more distant and less friendly image.[3] CBS repaired Rather's image, along with his ratings, by dressing him in sweaters that made him look "warmer" and less aloof.

Even the pace and mood of a day are captured by the news. Compare the slow, leisurely feel of the Sunday newspaper with the frantic pace —intensified by constant reminders of the exact time of day—of a week-day "rip and read" newscast on an all-news radio station. When people tune into the late-night local television news, it is no accident that they encounter a lighter, slower-paced format than the one used in the early evening news. It has become a law of the late-night news to close with an upbeat feature story that sends people off to bed reassured that, despite its problems, the world is still a safe and positive place.

The news has invaded everyday life to the point that it has become associated with things that people build their identities around, including self-image, status concerns, and sense of community. For example, a leading national news magazine ran an advertising campaign that equated reading the magazine with social respect, prestige, and personal competence. A major national newspaper devoted to business and economic affairs suggested that a subscription was a sign of good business sense and future career success. Local television news programs emphasize, both in advertising and program formats, the display of local symbols, landmarks, and themes of community pride. Viewers are encouraged to see the local TV news as a caring and watchful eye on the community they love.

The integration of news with everyday life is not just a one-way street. Not only are news forms responsive to individual life styles, but the news can also shape the pace and concerns of social life. It is easy and appealing for people to get caught up in the real-life dramas that unfold on the world stage. There seems to be a steady stream of long-playing news events such as wars, government scandals, economic crises, social changes, and political conflicts. These news "serials" can capture the attention and shape the emotions of the public.

When society becomes captivated by one of these sagas, it is hard to tell whether the news is a reflection of social life or whether the pace and mood of daily life are set by the news. For example, when the government corruption scandal "Watergate" reached its dramatic climax with the implication of President Nixon and all his top aides, millions of Americans became addicted to the daily media installments. One report on the Watergate audience of 1973 indicated that average Americans adjusted their lives to the year-long media spectacle:

... contrary to any picture of middle Americans tending their lawns and dialing out on the news, our panels paid close—even avid—attention to the Watergate scandals throughout the summer .... The blue-collar workers on the second shift at the Delco-Remy plant in Anderson, Ind., ... spent the day watching the televised Ervin committee hearings ... and then discussed Watergate at work.... [O]ne Portland business executive delayed going to his office until the morning hearings adjourned around 12:30 Washington time (9:30 on the West Coast). ... [I]n western Massachusetts, of ten panelists, seven read about Watergate daily in the newspapers and four watched the hearings regularly, especially the rebroadcasts at night on public television. Attention to the hearings was unexpectedly high among Nixon voters. In the engineering department of a large manufacturing plant in Dayton, there was only one McGovern voter in a group of 17 men holding managerial and foremen jobs; but a large majority of the group followed and approved of the hearings.[4]

A similar social preoccupation with the news occurred when Iranian rebels stormed the U.S. embassy in Tehran in 1979 and held the occupants captive. The media launched a 444-day series of dramatic updates on the situation. Even though there was very little "news" to report each day, the story continued to develop. As the unchanging political circumstances became monotonous, the focus of journalistic attention began to shift to the "home front." The news audience was bombarded with human interest stories of hometown vigils, public displays of concern, and Christmas back home with the hostages' families.

The human interest stories quickly became self-perpetuating news, with little or no connection to the political importance of the actual situation. It was as though a closed-circuit camera had been turned on the entire country. Millions of anonymous Americans became media stars for a day through their participation in patriotic rallies and demonstrations. The attention paid to these rallies spawned more and more of them, creating an always available formula news story. The saturation of the news with stories about public concern produced a saturation of society with more displays of public concern. It became impossible to attend a sporting event, a concert, or a public meeting without hearing something about the hostages. The proliferation of public concern added credibility to the increasingly standardized news stories, while the news stories fed on the diffusion of concern about the hostages.[5]

Stories like the hostage crisis and Watergate show how easily the news can capture the social imagination. Moreover, as the hostage crisis indicates, this captivation may have little to do with any objective properties of an event. As we shall see in the coming pages, these lessons apply even to news in its more mundane forms of government pronouncements, daily disasters, and heartwarming, real-life melodramas. Although the news appeals effectively to diverse sectors of the public, there is an underlying uniformity to the political messages it transmits. Recognizing the narrow range of content packaged in a broad range of communication styles is a key to understanding mass media news.

News Content: Messages for the Masses

Our expectations about the quality of public information are rather high. Most of us grew up with history books full of journalistic heroism in the name of truth and free speech. We learned that the American Revolution was inspired by the political rhetoric of the underground press and by printers' effective opposition to the British Stamp Act. The lesson from the trial of Peter Zenger has endured through time: The truth is not libelous. The goal of these and many other history-book journalists was as unswerving as it was noble: to guarantee for the American people the most accurate, objective, comprehensive, coherent, illuminating, and independent reporting of political events.

Somewhere along the line there have been some unfortunate substitutions for those laudable goals. In the real news, the journalistic balance falls more toward personalized, emotional reporting than toward the documentation of objective conditions. In place of illuminating analyses and explanations, there is an opposing emphasis on drama and action. Instead of displaying coherence and continuity, most stories fail to point out political changes, issue linkages, or historical patterns. Perhaps most important, the news avoids wide-ranging coverage of diverse viewpoints and experiences in favor of extensive coverage of official positions and mainstream perspectives. This preoccupation with "normalcy" creates the impression that there are few serious alternatives to mainstream politics and life styles.

These criticisms are not new. In fact, there is a sizable literature that reads like an inventory of problems and failings with the news.[6] Fortunately, a blow-by-blow review of this literature is unnecessary due to the remarkable degree of consensus among the critics. Virtually all the reported failings of the news can be summarized under four general categories. According to the majority of the critics, mass media news tends to be personalized, dramatized, fragmented, and normalized. It is important to be able to recognize each of these news characteristics in action.

Personalized News

In place of emphasizing the "big picture" surrounding important issues and events, news coverage often looks at the microcosm. The focus on the human angles of major stories can reduce the most monumental of events to terms of small proportion. Social forces are often represented through private experiences. Economic analyses are frequently reduced to reports of isolated financial successes and failures. Individual political actors often overshadow the issues they represent.

The personalization of the news is accomplished primarily by building stories around the human actors in events. This human focus may be interesting, but it often obscures the most important features of events, most notably, the workings of political processes, power relations, and economic forces. The invitation to respond on a human emotional level to major events not only distorts the events but diminishes the usefulness of any factual information news reports may contain. If the focus of an interpretation is on the soap-opera melodramas surrounding political personalities, the significance of more general social, political, or economic information becomes unclear or distorted.

The personal emotional appeal of a news story can be magnified further by the use of story angles based on psychological themes of security and reassurance. The news is filled with images of threat, fear, conflict, uncertainty, catastrophe, surprise, and reassurance. The use of such psychological themes represents the implicit reporting policy in most news organizations. So important is the private, individualized appeal of the news that it has even been written down as formal policy in at least one organization, as indicated by this memo from an executive producer of ABC news to his staff:

> The evening News, as you know, works on elimination. We can't include everything. As criteria for what we do include, I suggest the following for a satisfied viewer: (1) "Is my world, nation, and city safe?" (2) "Is my home and family safe?" (3) "If they are safe, then what has happened in the past 24 hours to help make that world better?" (4) "What has happened in the past 24 hours to help us cope better?"[7]

The personalized content of the news fits comfortably with the personalized styles of news delivery discussed earlier. In fact, the news is becoming increasingly like an intimate conversation between friends, where a message geared to personal concerns is delivered by a caring and respected messenger. It is no accident that a key ingredient of "life style news" is the image of the columnist, reporter, or anchor person who delivers the story. Journalists' personal images can create psychological bonds between audiences and their sources of news. Even though the news may be much the same across different programs or papers, the style of the journalist can affect credibility, interest, and understanding on the part of the audience. As a result, television, radio, and even newspapers have begun to emphasize the personalities of reporters. These efforts to get people to identify with the form of the news further personalizes the whole communication process. When radio and television stations begin to advertise their news programs with flashy commercials featuring the attractive people who read and report the stories, it is hard to distinguish serious informational programming from star-oriented entertainment fare. When print journalists become talk-show regulars and movie idols (as in the case of *Washington Post* reporters Bob Woodward and Carl Bernstein following their Watergate exploits), it becomes hard to separate what is said from who said it. This trend toward personalized reporting is likely to grow as the media rely more and more on the advice of professional news consultants. These "news doctors," like Philip McHugh of the influential firm McHugh and Hoffman, regard personalization of both content and delivery as the best way to sell the news: "There has to be an emphasis on human interest and human beings. You have to have an anchorman who can establish rapport with the audience. ... It takes a very special kind of personality."[8]

Examples of personalized coverage of events can be found in virtually any paper, magazine, or broadcast. Consider, for instance, a *Wall Street Journal* report on a government decision to terminate a large-scale public employment program. Despite the numerous "big picture" social, political, and economic themes that could have been used to frame the report, the opening paragraph of the story was this one:

> SAN FRANCISCO – As the chill, first light breaks on a Haight-Ashbury curbside, a street sweeper stops to gather the gutter's yield of leaves, litter, and dog waste. "This job's the best thing ever happened to a poor man," he says. "It's feeding babies. When it's over, I'll be putting cardboard in my little girl's shoes, like my mama did me."[9]

Although there is a journalistic law that stories should be organized with the most important information first and the least important facts last, the article made no mention of large-scale social, political, or economic implications of the program cuts until paragraphs 8, 9, and 10, and these brief passages were followed immediately by a return to the heart-rending story of the street sweeper's fate. Are we to infer from the proliferation of such stories that personal angles have replaced broader concerns as the most important information in the news?

The coverage of even the most important political events suggests that personal themes have, indeed, attained first place on the list of reporting priorities. As Paletz and Entman observed, "Prime news generally involves prominent, powerful people in action, or, more desirable from the media's point of view, in conflict."[10] A typical case in point was the press coverage of Ronald Reagan's first year in office. During that year, Reagan initiated many domestic and foreign policies of great national and international importance. However, the news formula that quickly emerged in most of the stories about those historic actions was the theme of whether Reagan was personally "winning" or "losing" in his battles with Congress, the bureaucracy, business leaders, and foreign governments. This theme reduced momentous political issues to engrossing but trivial questions about Reagan's personal power, his political "scorecard," and his risks of public embarrassment. The personal focus on Reagan so dominated the news that he was able to manipulate and enhance his news coverage simply by emphasizing his personal stake in major policy decisions. When he began defining his policies as tests of personal power, the news was locked into a familiar vicious cycle of the sort described earlier in the hostage crisis: A news theme had become artificially injected into real life, thereby creating the semblance of credibility for future coverage based on that theme.

A typical example of this personalization of political news was the reporting of Reagan's controversial "AWACS deal." AWACS is an acronym for a sophisticated U.S. Air Force radar and battle command aircraft. The Reagan administration proposed selling this plane, along with a large package of weaponry, to Saudi Arabia. The Senate had to approve such a sale, and many senators raised objections about selling sophisticated military equipment to an unpredictable nation in a volatile area of the world. There were, indeed, many serious political questions that could have dominated news coverage: Would the sale unbalance an already unstable region? How could the administration guarantee that the equipment would not be used for offensive purposes? What would keep the Saudi Arabians from showing top-secret U.S. technology to their ally, the Soviet Union? Would the sale alienate Israel, whose cooperation was vital to American efforts to settle long-standing disputes in the region? Was this all a thinly disguised power ploy designed to gain future U.S. control of precious oil fields?

Although some attention was paid to these important questions, the bulk of press coverage quickly fell into a personalistic formula. To begin with, the story became reduced to the "AWACS affair," even though AWACS was just one part of a larger arms package and even though the major political issues went well beyond the sale of a particular kind of military equipment. The focus on AWACS fit nicely with the personal theme of the President winning or losing, since the eventual vote in the Senate hinged on the sale of the airplane. The fact that the Senate vote revolved around the plane itself also had more to do with personalistic factors than with larger issues. It seems that several important senators had been embarrassed. Several years earlier they had gone on public record in support of this "highly sophisticated" aircraft that was now being billed by defense experts for purposes of the sale as a piece of old technology that would be of little use to Soviet spies. Thus the distorted emphasis on the AWACS vote in the Senate conveniently narrowed the whole issue to its purest personal form: the clash of individual power and human egos at the highest levels of government. The measure of this power and face-saving was the simplistic matter of how the Senate would vote.

The emergence of this classic news formula was no accident. Long before AWACS came to its dramatic conclusion with a narrow, eleventh-hour Reagan victory, a sage Washington observer had predicted that the larger issues would be lost in the preoccupation with the personalities involved. Peter Osnos, the national editor for the *Washington Post*, saw the early signs that AWACS had all the makings of a "Great Washington Drama."[11] It involved powerful figures locked in mortal combat. Power and reputations were on the line. There would be fascinating political maneuvering to report as the issue made its way through the formal processes of government. Moreover, there would be a guaranteed moment of climax (the vote) in which either possible outcome would be equally exciting (namely, Reagan would either "win" or "lose").

True to its self-fulfilling form, the AWACS saga headlined the news for over a month. The story gained prominence as it appeared that Reagan would lose his first political battle. However, in a last-minute session of wheeling and dealing, the President put everything on the line—and won! Not surprisingly, the last installment of this news serial placed the overwhelming emphasis on the personal aspect of the issue. Here is a sampling of how various news outlets presented the last chapter of the story.

> *A local TV newscast from a big-city CBS affiliate station:*
> Local Anchorperson Opens Program: "Good Evening. President Reagan's AWACS deal gets Senate approval."
> Cut to the program introduction and return to the anchorperson: "Now it's on to the next battle for the Reagan administration. President Reagan has won his toughest battle since taking office. It was a down-to-the-wire, come-from-behind win. . . ."
> Cut to a report from CBS national correspondent Leslie Stahl, who does a voice-over report on a videotape showing Reagan's top political aides tallying the votes during the Senate roll call. She tells the viewers that the top aides who engineered the big win had vowed not to "gloat" over the victory. The report ended with Stahl saying that Reagan's first act after the victory was to call his wife, Nancy, and tell her the good news.
> Cut to a report on the favorable impact the sale would have on a local aircraft company.
> Cut to a network report showing a parallel negative effect on the British aircraft business that had hoped to sell its plane to Saudi Arabia if the AWACS deal fell through.

Cut (at last, and, therefore, least) to CBS Israeli correspondent Bob Fall reporting briefly from Jerusalem to say that the effects of the AWACS sale on U.S.–Israeli relations could be negative.[12]

NBC network television 9 p.m. evening news update following the final game of the world series:
Anchorperson opens with a recap of the just-completed, come-from-behind series victory of the Los Angeles Dodgers.

After announcing himself as John Shubek reporting from L.A., he continues: 'Another Californian came from behind to win a big one today. The Californian, of course, is Ronald Reagan, who received a vote of 52–48 from the Senate on the AWACS arms sale to Saudi Arabia."[13]

ABC network television "Nightline" program, 11:30 p.m.:
Program opens with dramatic close-up of the host, who announces, "The President wins on the AWACS sale, but what happens next?"

Following the introduction of the program, the host returns with: "Good evening. The President put his own prestige on the line and he won. He lobbied hard all day with key senators. . . ."

Shots of senators who changed their minds on the issue. Followed by shots of Senate Minority Leader Alan Cranston on the phone "trying hard to hold his opposition coalition together."

Cut to White House with shots of aides tallying the votes.

Cut back to the Senate chamber with comments from elated supporters and dejected opponents after the vote.

Cut to interview with a senator who stresses that he voted for the President, not for AWACS.

Finally, the host asks the question "What next?" and introduces a series of political observers who discuss the political consequences of the arms sale.[14]

A big-city newspaper:
Banner headline: PRESIDENT WINS AWACS
Opening two paragraphs of story under headline:

WASHINGTON – President Reagan, displaying extraordinary muscle, scored a major foreign policy victory yesterday as the Senate voted 52–48 to allow the sale of AWACS radar planes and other military hardware to Saudi Arabia.

The tally that defeated a resolution to disapprove the $8.5 billion package represented a stunning turnaround of Senate opinion. Friend and foe alike said Reagan's personal persuasion was the crucial ingredient in building the winning coalition behind the largest single foreign military sale in U.S. history.[15]

The Political Effects of Personalized News

When issues are reported in the fashion of the AWACS saga, it is easy to think that private political fortunes *are* the important issues at stake. The focus of attention on actors rather than their actions is all the more compelling because of the dramatic nature of human interest stories. Dry political analysis of causes and consequences may be more important, but it is surely less exciting. The introduction of gripping human melodrama into a story creates the illusion of importance even when, as in the AWACS case, the truly important considerations have been abandoned.

The tendency to personalize the news gives the news audience a distorted view of power, issues, and consequences. As Paletz and Entman have concluded: "Power seems to be understood in a limited sense by the media. . . . Stories emphasize the surface appearances, the furious sounds and fiery sights of battle, the well-known or colorful personalities involved—whatever is dramatic. Underlying causes and actual impacts are little noted nor long remembered."[16]

The personalized view of politics gives people little, if any, grasp of political processes or power structures. Without a grasp of these things it is virtually impossible to understand how the political system really works. As a result, the political world becomes a mystical realm populated by actors who either have the political "force" on their side or do not. The mysterious possession or loss of power further encourages the audience to abandon political analysis in favor of casting their political fates with the hero of the moment.

The world of personalized politics is thus a fantasy world. Like any fantasy world of play, sport, or fiction, it can involve people intensely on the basis of catharsis, escape, hope, or sheer entertainment. Unfortunately, the world of personalized politics is one in which meaningful political understanding and effective political access are limited severely. Aided by the news, American politics is a world in which today's heroes are tomorrow's fools. The primary substance in this world is the occasional moment when the public, fooled again, rises up and banishes the latest fool to make way for the newest elected hero.

Most of us are aware at some level of an emptiness in the world of personalized politics. People who have lost at the hands of the political system are cynical and frustrated, often without really knowing why. People who have gained from the system are often blindly supportive, again without really knowing why. Both winners and losers tend to praise or blame supposedly powerful individuals (or stereotypes like "liberals," "conservatives," "environmentalists," or "bureaucrats") because those individuals, after all, have been represented, day in and day out, as the moving forces in the political system. Cynicism, frustration, or blind loyalty may be the only long-term responses to the personalization of politics, but the short term offers continuous promise of renewed hope: new heroes, new promises, and all packaged in engrossing political dramas.

Dramatized News

The potential for drama (even contrived, self-fulfilling drama like the AWACS vote) is a virtual guarantee that an event will become a major news story. It is no secret that reporters and editors search for events with dramatic properties and then emphasize those properties in their reporting. Consider, for example, the following policy memo from the executive news producer of a major television network to his editors and reporters:

> Every news story should, without any sacrifice of probity or responsibility, display the attributes of fiction, of drama. It should have structure and conflict, problem and denouement, rising action and falling action, a beginning, a middle, and an end. These are not only the essentials of drama; they are the essentials of narrative.[17]

The weight of such evidence has led one pair of observers to conclude that: "Drama is a defining characteristic of news. An event is particularly newsworthy if it has some elements of a dramatic narrative.... American officials held hostage in the far off but journalistically accessible land of Iran provide a particularly strident example."[18] Indeed, the hostage crisis is a good example of an event that was the object of sustained news coverage because it contained so many dramatic angles, almost all of which involved personalized themes and plots.

Just as the AWACS and hostage stories virtually wrote themselves once their dramatic outlines were determined, most stories fall into their own, almost subconscious dramatic formulas. Robert Darnton, a top reporter for the *New York Times*, told of his early problems as a journalist before he had learned to parse the dramatic highlights from the dull details of most stories. On one of his early assignments on the city desk of a small town, he wrote a story of a bicycle stolen from a paper boy. The story was rejected by his editor. A colleague suggested a much more dramatic version involving the boy's love for the bike, his trauma following the theft, and his Horatio Alger–like scheme to pay for a new one. Upon checking the new plot against the facts, Darnton decided that reality was close enough to the dramatized version to write the story—a story that was published in his paper.[19]

Lewis Lapham tells of similar experiences in his early days as a reporter. He notes how he marveled at the ease with which the senior reporter in the city room "wrote the accounts of routine catastrophe."[20] Finally, the old reporter's secret came out:

> In the drawer, with a bottle of bourbon and the manuscript of the epic poem he had been writing for twenty years, he kept a looseleaf notebook filled with stock versions of maybe fifty or sixty common newspaper texts. These were arranged in alphabetical order (fires, homicides, ship collisions, etc.) and then further divided into sub-categories (fires—one-, two-, and three-

alarm; warehouse; apartment building, etc.). The reporter had left blank spaces for the relevant names, deaths, numbers, and street addresses. As follows: "A _____ alarm fire swept through _____ at_____ St. yesterday afternoon, killing _____ people and causing _____ in property damage."[21]

This preoccupation with drama makes it hard to draw the line between journalists as reporters of fact and creators of fiction. After making the standard observation that drama is a requirement for a major news story, Paletz and Entman go on to observe that some stories deficient in their own "high drama" may "have drama grafted on. Journalists have been known to highlight if not concoct conflict and to find characters to symbolize its different sides. One reason: to attract an audience that is thought to have little patience for the abstract, the technical, the ambiguous, the uncontroversial."[22]

We shall see later on that the public is not as simpleminded as the news experts assume. But this is beside the point. Nowhere in journalism texts is news defined as "whatever the audience wants, no matter how contrived or irrelevant." News, at least in theory, is supposed to inform people, not merely entertain them. The trend toward ever more dramatic and entertaining news may mean that a new form of mass communication is emerging. This evolving communication form may still go by the term "news," but it would be a serious mistake to assume that the traditional meanings of that term still apply.

The dramatization of public events has gained increasing acceptance with the advent of the "news doctors" who have promoted successfully the "action news" format. Virtually every major media market now has a news program called "Action News" or "Eyewitness News." Part of the action format calls for changes in the pace, delivery, scenery, and casting of the program. The action focus also makes direct inroads into story content and presentation. Consider, for example, the multitude of ways in which a routine event like a murder can be covered. At one extreme, a murder can be reported analytically in order to show how various aspects of the crime reflect social problems known to be linked with violent crime (problems such as poverty, family violence, unemployment, alcoholism, social instability, or prison system failures). Such reporting angles are seldom used in action news programs because they contradict the action philosophy of the news doctors. TV and radio stations in competitive media markets tend to follow the costly advice of news consultants like Frank Magid, who is reported to endorse the example of a murder story built around the dramatic effects of the camera retracing the route of the killer as he stalked his victim. Such reporting, according to Magid, has the virtue of making you feel "as if you were really there."[23]

As the preoccupation with action news grows, dramatization becomes a routine practice. For example, many stations have purchased expensive helicopters, airplanes, and remote transmission equipment to enhance their action news image. Such equipment usually becomes a visible feature of the station's news coverage, both to justify its expense and to ensure that the news program lives up to its action news advertising. As a result of this built-in bias in favor of action reporting, a new breed of news stories has begun to appear: stories that have less to do with the importance or meaning of an event than with the capacity to use costly equipment and convey images of drama and action.[24]

A case in point involves a big-city TV station that had consistently placed last in the local news ratings battles. After hiring one of the news doctor firms, the station adopted the action news format, complete with a new title, music, cast, set, helicopter, and advertising campaign (featuring, of course, dramatic shots of Channel 7's new "Chopper 7" going after the hottest news). The station quickly won first place in the ratings war, but may have lost its chance to win any serious news game. Following the switch to action news, a typical evening's newscast began with the report that a U.S. Navy jet from a local base had crashed on a training flight across the country. Prior to the advent of action news, the story would never have opened a newscast (for a variety of reasons, among them that the crash involved no fatalities, it occurred across the country, the plane's base was some 60 miles from the city, and there had been no official navy reaction to the crash). However, the incident created an opportunity to fly to the air base in Chopper 7 and transmit a live report from the runway where the plane took off earlier in the day. The report consisted of little more than meaningless, but very dramatic, shots of other planes taking off from the airstrip. Despite the virtual absence of meaning in the story, the created image was a dramatic one, and the advertised promise of "action news" was once again fulfilled by having the lead story of the nightly news captioned with "Live report from Chopper 7."

The Political Effects of Dramatized News

As the above example indicates, the most obvious effect of dramatization is to trivialize news content. In place of unswerving attention to major events and problems, there is an increasing tendency to substitute manufactured drama. Even when the drama may reflect an actual feature of the situation, as in the case of the AWACS vote, the preoccupation with drama often distracts attention from any broad or enduring political significance the event may have had. As Tuchman has observed so cogently, the action imperative feeds on events that have some rapidly developing action to report. As a result, chronic social problems and long-standing political issues often go unreported because they develop too slowly.[25]

Events that have become separated from their political contexts in order to emphasize isolated dramatic aspects are subject to distortion and misinterpretation. When the political world is turned into a television drama, people may think they understand an issue when, in fact, their understanding is based on a mixture of fantasy, fiction, and myth. Under these circumstances, according to Lapham, the political world becomes sheer abstraction, and

> . . . we exhaust ourselves in passionate arguments about things that few of us have ever seen. We talk about the third world as if it were a real place rather than a convenient symbol, about the gears of the national economy as if it were as intelligible as the gears on a bicycle. People become lifelong enemies because they disagree about the military strategy of the Soviet Union; on further investigation it generally turns out that neither antagonist speaks Russian or has been to Russia.[26]

Even though dramatized news both trivializes and confuses the meaning of political issues, the rush to the action news format continues. Just a few days after the assassination of Egyptian President Anwar Sadat in 1981, a leading radio station in a major U.S. city sent a team of reporters to the scene. Saturation advertising on television, radio, and newspapers promised that the team would reveal the answers to all the "burning questions" about the "explosive" Middle East. The answers, it turned out, resembled the typical news stereotypes about Arab-Israeli hostilities, strong political personalities, and U.S.–Soviet struggles for dominance in the region. Nevertheless, the region had somehow become more "explosive" with Sadat's death. The evidence for the use of this dramatic metaphor? The presence of a team of action reporters covering the situation, of course.

In a world where political events are already far removed from the immediate experience of the average person, news dramas may push political consciousness permanently into the realm of fiction. For example, a big-city television station produced an expensive and much advertised documentary special on violent crime. The newspaper and television ads were dominated by the horror-movie use of the word *fear* that seared the page and dripped from the TV screen. True to its advertising, the program presented numerous examples of particularly violent crimes and showed how typical people reacted to them. When the news adopts the images of popular drama and literature, it is little wonder that people begin to confuse reality and fantasy. As the following personal statement of a newspaper columnist indicates, our own lives become dramatized:

> Is it possible for a woman to walk alone, footsteps echoing through the night city, without feeling as if she's performing in a Brian DePalma movie? I can't. I've been conditioned into DePalma-style reflexes: twitches and eye

rolls, in response to any unlikely sight or sound. What is that shape moving shadowlike in the alley? Is that a garbage bag or a man hunkered down in the service doorway? If I venture out alone after midnight, I enter an atmosphere as different from the everyday world as if I've gone under water. I can hear my own breathing, the hammering of my heart, the clickety-clack of my heels on the pavement. Unescorted, I am accompanied by fear, chaperoned by phantoms of my own imagination. Why has that man changed direction, just as I've turned the corner? Is that he now walking behind me?[27]

Fragmented News

Columnist Russell Baker once parodied the typical newscast in the following terms:

> Meanwhile, in Washington, the Carter Administration was reported today as firemen still sifted through the ruins of a six-alarm blaze in Brooklyn that left two Congressmen, who were said to have accepted cash contributions from Korean agents, despite their fifth defeat in a row at the hands of the Boston Celtics. . . .
>
> Seventeen were dead and scores injured by the testimony that two Senators, whom he declined to name, rioted in the streets of Cairo following her son's expulsion from school for shooting a teacher who had referred to him in the easy-going style of the Carter White House, as exemplified by the dispute over the B-1 bomber.[28]

Some news critics would argue that Baker's satire is not so far from reality. Edwin Diamond tells the story of a network news producer who visited a seminar at M.I.T. devoted to television news. The producer proudly showed a videotape of a recent "analytical" report on the economy. Diamond describes the report and his students' reaction:

> There was the anchor wishing us good evening; cut to the Washington reporter with the latest inflation bad news; then quickly three consumer reports from around the country; then a U.S. map with graphics showing cost of living rates; back to the anchor and then the Washington reporter, followed by tape and sound "bites"—15 second quotes—from congressional leaders and cabinet officers. Finally, a Wall Street reaction . . . and then break for commercial. In all, no more than three minutes had elapsed.
>
> As the various tape, sound, and graphics parts in the economics package gave way to each other, the producer snapped her fingers and whispered "hit it . . ." right in time with each element. She was proud of the network handiwork, but students in the classroom shot up their hands. What was that all about? What did it mean? What were you trying to tell us about the economy? . . . When we all watched the videotape once again from the point of view of the audience—people who know little about the effort that goes into the smooth mingling of tape and sound videofonts and slides, and

care even less—we had to admit that it was difficult to grasp, sort out and understand the news somewhere underneath all the production.[29]

As the above example illustrates, action news often sacrifices length and detail in favor of pace, change of scene, and personalization. The resulting news collages, called "clusters" in radio and television, contain many images with few coherent connections.[30] Similar fragmentation effects are achieved in newspapers by jumping back and forth between interviews, actors, scenes, factual information, and plots. Recall, for example, how the newspaper article on the elimination of the government job program required the reader to make the leap from one isolated personal case to the broad economic implications involved.

Fragmentation can occur both within and between stories. Although not all stories suffer from internal incoherence, almost all stories suffer from the absence of meaningful connections to each other. An event reported one way today may be presented in another way tomorrow. Events that result from the same political or economic forces are often treated as though they were independent. Long-term trends and historical patterns are seldom made part of the news. In short, even though political, social, and economic events tend to fit together into broad patterns, the news pictures them as fragmented. In place of seeing a coherent world with clear historical trends, the public sees a world driven into chaos by seemingly arbitrary and mysterious forces. For example, during his first year in office, Ronald Reagan successfully dismantled nearly forty years of government social protection programs. The cuts in every social service and public protection area were awesome. Yet there were no headlines proclaiming that *Reagan Dismantles 40 Years of Government Reforms*. Instead, the dismantling of each program was announced separately, often days apart and frequently dwarfed by the ongoing crises of state and economy. In looking at the *Wall Street Journal* coverage of just five of the dozens of Reagan dismantling efforts, we find that two received front-page coverage (Social Security cuts and the termination of the CETA program). A proposal to close the Consumer Product Safety Commission was given about four inches on page 5 in one issue, and a longer article on page 48 in another. A plan to shut off welfare to families of strikers was relegated to page 6. The decision to stop tracing the ownership transfers of firearms was covered on page 31. The impact and linkages among these issues were further diminished by the fact that the stories were spread over a period of two months.[31] What stopped journalists from announcing these and other actions as a major and significant trend once the pattern became evident? Trends do not conform to the narrow definition of daily news unless, of course, they are in the interest of governments or interest groups to announce. More important, trends seldom contain the dramatic elements of a good story. Headlining trends and linkages would require placing information in analytically useful forms, a function that the news is ill equipped to perform.

The Political Effects of Fragmentation

There are, of course, numerous "good reasons" for such bad reporting. Journalism's hallowed prohibitions against commentary and interpretation result in the face-value representation of separate events, no matter how interrelated they may be. Moreover, press releases from official news sources seldom take pains to point out inconsistencies, complex relations, or other "big picture" aspects of events. These incremental strategies of propagandists are rewarded by the journalistic preoccupation with "daily news," which means that the news slate is wiped clean each day. News update sections are relegated to the back of the newspaper and saved for "slow news days" in radio and television broadcasts. The imperatives for drama and action further separate stories from one another. Since dramatic formats contain their own plot and resolution elements, linkages between these "news capsules" can reduce their impact and confuse their plots. In fact, connections between news stories can raise the unsettling idea that nothing should be taken at face value, that behind every story there is a still larger story.[32] It is an unfortunate by-product of using stories as the basic units of news reporting that linkages evoke unpleasant images of political conspiracies or journalistic attempts to obfuscate simple issues. By contrast, other forms of presenting information, such as ideologies and theories, use connections to simplify explanations and enhance meaning.

Due to the internal incoherence of cluster reporting and the external isolation of stories, the news audience is seldom given a fully assembled picture of a political situation. It is no wonder that public opinion studies have shown that most people have trouble thinking in abstract, logically integrated ways about political issues. An inventory of findings from public opinion research sounds like a list of the effects of news fragmentation. The average person has trouble stating clear positions on issues; most people tend to remember few facts about important issues; the majority of people see few connections between issues; and many people change their opinions easily about issues.[33] The parallels between news fragmentation and public opinion characteristics suggest that the public's true failing has been to follow the news and take it seriously.

Public confusion may not be the worst effect of news fragmentation. Since events are often isolated from their larger political contexts, audiences may be led at times to draw clear but misguided conclusions. The failure to report an event's political context created such grounds for possible misinterpretation in a CBS radio news report. Here is how CBS reported a Federal Trade Commission decision to drop a major antitrust action against the eight largest oil companies:

NEWSCASTER: The government has dropped an eight-year-old antitrust case against big oil. The Federal Trade Commission doesn't address the merits of the case, but says pursuing it is no longer in the public interest. It's too complex, says the FTC—and too far from being resolved. It was first brought in 1973—charging the nation's eight biggest oil companies with anticompetitive practices. A spokeswoman at Chevron says the dismissal is only proper.

CHEVRON SPOKESPERSON: The dismissal of the case reflects the mutual interest of everyone, the Federal Trade Commission, the eight respondent oil companies, and the general public. We have felt strongly from the beginning of the case that it was not soundly based in fact or in economics, and we are glad to see now that the commission has come around to that point of view, and now agrees that no public purpose would be served by continued prosecution of the case.

NEWSCASTER: The FTC says—from now on—cases involving the oil industry will be handled in a more focused proceeding.[34]

It would be easy to interpret this report to mean that the antitrust suit was dropped for lack of cause, and that the oil companies had been right all along. This interpretation, of course, is the one contained in the statement by the spokesperson from Chevron. However, an entirely different interpretation would have emerged had the report included an important piece of contextual information. The FTC suit began under a presidential administration that supported more vigorous antitrust action. The suit was dropped after the election of a President who opposed most antitrust action and ordered government regulatory agencies to be more friendly and cooperative with big business. This political context suggests that the decision to drop the suit was a political calculation having little to do with the "complexity" or "merits" of the case. The fragmentation of the report thus favored a misleading and politically loaded interpretation over a more accurate and politically revealing one. It is not clear which effect of news fragmentation is worse: diminishing the capacity to grasp issues at all, or increasing the chance of grasping issues incorrectly.

Normalized News

As the antitrust report illustrates, official sources often get in the last word in a news story. In fact, most news stories reserve for official sources the first, the last, and many of the words in between. Much of the daily news is devoted to official actions and reactions. It is convenient that there is a never-ending supply of official news because news organizations need a huge volume of news every day. The public relations branches of government, interest groups, and industry are dedicated to filling up this daily "news hole."

There are, of course, many reports of the activities of socially and politically deviant actors such as strikers, protest groups, or splinter parties. Virtually all reports of such actors tend to fall into one or more of the following categories:[35]

1. *Reports of lawbreaking, violence, or distasteful behavior that tend to discredit the actors involved.* For example, environmental groups may publicize their opposition to nuclear power plants by disrupting work or occupying the grounds. News reports that associate the group with illegal tactics, arrests, and criminal prosecution may damage the credibility of the group and its cause.

2. *Reports that balance a deviant perspective with an official reaction in opposition.* For example, many political organizations during the 1960s claimed that the FBI had attempted to sabotage their organizations and harass their members. These charges were always accompanied by denials from the FBI, the Department of Justice, the President, and other authoritative sources. It was not until years later that FBI officials admitted to congressional investigators that they had engaged in illegal activities against political groups. By that time the issue was dead.

3. *Reports on the positive activities of a group that quickly fade from the news, implying that the group and its goals were of little consequence.* For example, many grass-roots groups receive initial press coverage when they announce their intentions to tackle a political problem. However, such groups usually lack the money and public relations skills required to keep their concerns before the public over the long haul.

Even when reporters find themselves in situations where they might turn up new angles and new points of view, there is a tendency to avoid such deviations from official perspectives.[36] For example, shortly after Ronald Reagan became President, there was a major "North-South" economic summit conference held in Mexico. The conference received a good deal of American press coverage both because it was Reagan's first serious diplomatic venture outside the country and because it was billed as a major forum for working out the economic crisis. Even though Reagan brought a huge press contingent with him, those reporters spent little time finding out how the other countries viewed the problems on the agenda. As one observer put it:

... Reagan brought an enormous White House press corps. If the spokesmen for the poorer countries thought that meant access to American media, which rarely discuss issues of development, they were in for a surprise. "We'll try to feed you as often as possible," Secretary of State Alexander Haig promised at an early briefing in the makeshift White House press room, situated in the basement of the hotel where most of the American reporters stayed. The Reagan Administration did feed the media, and many American journalists' accounts of what happened at [the conference] came straight from that official source. Some members of the White House press spent an entire week there without meeting a single foreign delegate.[37]

But what about the notorious attacks by the press on Presidents and other powerful leaders? Occasional instances of press criticism do stand out against the familiar pattern of official reporting. Even though these moments of judgmental journalism seem to suggest an independent press, they are, in fact, the exceptions that prove the rule of normalized news. Most news reports that seem critical of authority reflect one or more of the following properties:

1. *They are rare.* The comparatively small number of critical reports convey the impression that official positions are credible in the vast majority of cases.

2. *They are ritualized.* News criticisms tend to come at measured intervals, and they often have little to do with the substance of issues. For example, a study by Orr showed that presidential press conferences usually contain a fairly constant percentage of hostile questions regardless of the President or the issues of the day.[38] Moreover, press criticism rarely addresses the merits of policies or the substance of issues. Rather, criticism is confined largely to personal slips, blunders, embarrassments, or scandals. Such attacks create the posture of a critical press without involving journalists in discussions of political substance.[39]

3. *They are superficial.* When an official is criticized, the news treatment is generally personalistic, dramatized, and fragmented. As suggested above, criticisms tend to be personal rather than substantive, often centered on dramatic questions concerning personal integrity, power, winning and losing. Such questions lead to news fragmentation by confusing issues with personalities and further weakening linkages between issues.

A typical case that illustrates these properties of critical news is an NBC news special on Ronald Reagan's first year in the White House.[40] Typical of most critical news, the special was a rare moment of criticism following a long period of uncritical reporting of Reagan's activities. Also typical of the ritualized, superficial nature of most press criticism, the focus was on the person rather than the issues. This personal attack created the illusion of critical reporting without risking the introduction of much political substance or detailed analysis. Despite the use of such standard news formulas, it was hard for the viewer not to get caught up in the dramatic illusion that there was really something important going on. Reporters on the program went so far as to suggest that Reagan might not have understood the nature of the Presidency in some of his dealings with Congress. The host of the program interviewed the President and asked him, point-blank, to "comment" on reports from his own staff that he was not really aware of the details of most issues—in fact, some said he did not even understand most issues. Was it true, the interviewer asked audaciously, that the White House staff tried to prevent unrehearsed encounters between the President and the press because they often resulted in embarrassing statements?

Despite the sense of an almost ruthless attack, there was something missing: a serious look at Reagan's policies. In addition to violating the canons of personalization and dramatization, such an approach would have raised the uncomfortable question "where was the press with these criticisms when these same policies were being debated before Congress and the public?" Instead, the safe but impressive strategy adopted was to frame the program around questions of Reagan's "personal rating," his "score as President," and his "win/loss record."

The moral to this story is that appearances can be deceiving in news reporting. Although the NBC "White Paper" discussed above seemed to depart from an official position, it did nothing of the kind. By avoiding a serious and timely criticism of specific policies, the report did little to disrupt "normal" images of society and its problems. Even if the program had raised criticisms of specific issues, the formula for news criticism would have introduced them in the form of equally "normal" views held by members of the opposition party in Congress. In the end, press attacks on "officials" and their views are of little consequence, since both officials and mainstream views seem to be infinitely replaceable in American politics.

The standard journalistic treatment of officials and their positions is just one way in which the news presents the world in "normalized" terms. As mentioned earlier, journalists draw many of their story plots from the numerous subconscious dramatic themes of the culture—themes that clearly delimit good and bad, right and wrong, desirable and undesirable, normal and abnormal, the thinkable and the unthinkable. Such themes leave their marks on the news:

- A teacher's strike reported as a traditional wage dispute, thereby ignoring more pertinent issues of racism in the schools and political control of educational policy.[41]
- Extensive coverage of Poland's political struggle in 1981 and 1982

in which little effort was made to point out the profound differences between Polish and American workers, thereby creating false grounds for the American audience to become involved with the situation.[42]

- A report on China after Mao that used American stereotypes of progress and development to describe a "typical" Chinese family: "They chatter in eager, sometimes mirthful, manner about the improvements in their lives since Mr. Deng has been in power. Their sofa, TV, a coat of blue paint on the walls and partitions separating the living room from the eating area are all post-Mao additions."[43]

In short, the news takes us on a daily tour of the world-as-it-ought-to-be: a world filled with mainstream American values, and comforting images of authority and security. As if to affirm that nothing serious lies beyond these boundaries of normalized news, daily journalistic fare also contains a sampling of the truly bizarre: the wrecking crew that demolished the wrong building, the eccentric millionaire who left his entire estate to his cat, the confusion that resulted when a gang of robbers dressed as cops encountered a squad of cops dressed as robbers, or the travails of people who have adopted dolls as children and must find sensitive babysitters when they go on vacation.

The Political Effects of Normalized News

The main effect of normalized news is obvious: It narrows the range of acceptable, even "thinkable," models for political action. This narrowing effect often goes unnoticed because the news always seems filled with conflicts and competing viewpoints. Nevertheless, there is almost always a line drawn between legitimate and illegitimate dissent. For example, coverage of a respected member of the opposition political party disagreeing with the President will surely differ from the portrayal of disagreement by a radical opposition group. And just as surely as official opposition will be pictured more credibly, so will the content of official opposition fall within the range of acceptable, mainstream political ideas. Whether the official opposition comes from liberal or conservative channels, one thing will be certain: we will know the lines by heart. Mainstream political groups may disagree with one another bitterly, but no matter how aggressive their posturing, they suffer the common fate of being confined to the same stereotypical positions over time. There is irony in this general enslavement by stereotypes. Officials gain credibility by talking in stereotypes because it helps define their positions as official. Since official positions make the news more often, there is little incentive to say anything different or controversial. Thus the least newsworthy items dominate the news, conveniently minimizing the risks to powerful interests, and lamentably ignoring the interests of weaker actors.

It is not surprising that many powerful political and economic figures cling to simplistic and stereotypical views of important issues, at least in public. After all, it is not in the interest of the wealthy and successful to advocate ideas that would seriously alter the status quo. What is surprising is the apparent public acceptance of these political perspectives despite their past records of political failure. For example, a favorite "official" explanation of poverty and chronic unemployment is that some people just do not seem to have the motivation, discipline, and self-respect to acquire job skills and keep jobs. Every so often one of the parties will promote an employment program based on these assumptions. The program typically involves some sort of aid to unemployed persons coupled with various incentives to seek training and jobs. These programs have little, if any, effect on long-term employment rates or on the real causes of chronic unemployment. When such programs fail, their opponents can be expected to condemn the underlying political reasoning and to reintroduce their own favorite stereotypes about the problem. The supporters, however, typically do something strange. Instead of rejecting ideas that clearly do not work, they often cling all the more strongly to them. Failure of a program becomes proof of the assumptions on which it was based. Thus the employment program failed precisely because people were so unmotivated, undisciplined, and lacking in self-respect that they resisted the best efforts of the government to help them![44]

And so it goes. One set of failed solutions is succeeded by another, only to be replaced by the first. The important feature of this parade of political stereotypes is that it is kept alive by "official" news sources—people who are given the lion's share of news space. The tedium of this news cycle is alleviated somewhat by the shifting personalities and subtle dramatic differences in each political episode. Dramatization and personalization thus reward the attention of the news audience, even though the message is virtually constant. As a result of presenting political stereotypes in conjunction with emotional stimuli, the news becomes a means of reinforcing the narrow political images that dominate its content.

In view of these normalizing effects, it is doubtful that the news comes very close to its reputed function of presenting unvarnished political facts so that people can draw informed conclusions from them. It is closer to the mark to conclude that the news helps people confirm their favorite political truths because those truths form the implicit guidelines for selecting and writing news stories. As one critic observed, both the public and journalists are involved more in a process of creating convenient fictions than discovering convincing facts: "We are all engaged in the same enterprise, all of us caught up in the making of analogies and metaphors, all of us seeking evocations and representations of what we can recognize as appropriately human. Stories move from truths to facts, not the other way around. . . ."[45]

In this process of legitimizing a narrow range of political values (and the actors who endorse them) the news accomplishes another important end: It legitimizes itself. As mentioned earlier, claims about "objective" reporting rest on very shaky foundations. For every story angle highlighted, another goes unreported. For every source included, another is excluded. With each tightening of the plot line, meaningful connections to other issues and events become weakened. Every familiar theme or metaphor used in writing about an event obscures a potentially unique feature of the event. Even though it is impossible for the news to be objective, it is important that it seem objective. The appearance of objectivity depends heavily on the use of official sources and normalizing themes. The routine acceptance of official views helps to legitimize them, which in turn helps make the news seem objective. According to Tuchman:

> Challenging the legitimacy of offices holding centralized information dismantles the news net. If all of officialdom is corrupt, all its facts and occurrences must be viewed as alleged facts and alleged occurrences. . . . For example, if the institutions of everyday life are delegitimated, the facts tendered by the Bureau of Marriage Licenses would be suspect. One could no longer call that bureau to learn whether Robert Jones and Fay Smith had married. In sum, amassing mutually self-validating facts simultaneously accomplishes the doing of newswork and reconstitutes the everyday world of offices and factories, of politics and bureaucrats, of bus schedules and class rosters as historically given.[46]

The news is worth studying, as Tuchman suggests, because it plays a major part in creating the reality in which we live. Even though the news may be illusory, the world it helps legitimize is not. War is an ever-present possibility. Oppression is a fact of political life. Capricious economic cycles dictate the quality of existence. Many people accept these aspects of reality as inescapable tragedies of the human condition. A review of the effects of mass media news suggests that the "inevitability" of our existence is more a product of how that existence is communicated to us than it is the result of tragic human nature. The news world simply does not contain a vision of human alternatives; it presents, instead, a picture of an inescapable status quo.

Notes

1. The data on print media were drawn from *Editor and Publisher International Yearbook: 1982* (New York: Editor and Publisher, 1982), 1:305–70. The data on broadcast media can be found in the *Statistical Abstract of the United States, 1981* (Washington, D.C.: U.S. Department of Commerce, 1981), p. 564.

2. See, for example, Jay G. Blumler and Denis McQuail, *Television in Politics: Its Uses and Influences* (Chicago: University of Chicago Press, 1969); Lee B. Becker, "Two Tests of Media Gratifications: Watergate and the 1974 Election," *Journalism Quarterly* 53 (1976): 26–31; Mark R. Levy, "Television News Uses: A Cross-National Comparison," *Journalism Quarterly* 55 (Summer 1978): 334–37; and Mark R. Levy, "Watching TV News as Para-Social Activity," *Journal of Broadcasting* 23 (Winter 1979): 69–80.

3. Based on marketing studies of TV news personalities reported in Gerald M. Goldhaber, "The Charisma Factor: Why Dan Rather May Be in Trouble," *TV Guide*, 2 May 1981, pp. 4–6.

4. Edwin Diamond, "The Folks in the Boondocks: Challenging a Journalistic Myth," *Columbia Journalism Review*, November/December 1973, p. 58.

5. A fascinating historical study showing how events can take on a social life of their own is John William Ward's *Andrew Jackson: Symbol for an Age* (New York: Oxford University Press, 1955).

6. See, for example, Edward Jay Epstein, *News from Nowhere* (New York: Random House, 1973); Herbert Gans, *Deciding What's News* (New York: Vintage, 1979); Timothy Crouse, *The Boys on the Bus* (New York: Random House, 1972); Gaye Tuchman, *Making News* (New York: Free Press, 1978); Robert Darnton, "Writing News and Telling Stories," *Daedalus*, Spring 1975, pp. 175–97; Mark Fishman, *Manufacturing the News* (Austin: University of Texas Press, 1980); Todd Gitlin, *The Whole World Is Watching* (Berkeley: University of California Press, 1980); Harvey Molotch and Marilyn Lester, "News as Purposive Behavior," *American Sociological Review* 39 (1974): 101–12; Harvey Molotch and Marilyn Lester, "Accidental News: The Great Oil Spill," *American Journal of Sociology* 81 (1975): 235–60; Leon V. Sigal, *Reporters and Officials: The Organization and Politics of Newsmaking* (Lexington, Mass.: Heath, 1973); David L. Paletz and Robert M. Entman, *Media Power Politics* (New York: Free Press, 1981).

7. Reported in Paletz and Entman, *Media Power Politics*, p. 17.

8. Quoted in Edward W. Barrett, "Folksy TV News," *Columbia Journalism Review*, November/December 1973, p. 19.

9. *Wall Street Journal*, 17 June 1981, p. 1.

10. Paletz and Entman, *Media Power Politics*, pp. 16–17.

11. Osnos's observations were aired in an interview on the National Public Radio news program "Morning Edition" on 21 September 1981.

12. KIRO-TV, 11 p.m. news, Seattle, Wash., 28 October 1981.

13. NBC television network news update, 9 p.m. Pacific Time Zone, 28 October 1981.

14. ABC "Nightline," 11:30 p.m. Pacific Time Zone, 28 October 1981.

15. *Seattle Post-Intelligencer*, 29 October 1981, p. 1.
16. Paletz and Entman, *Media Power Politics*, p. 17.
17. Reported in Epstein, *News from Nowhere*, pp. 4–5. The existence of such a conscious statement of a defining characteristic of news is all the more remarkable considering the trouble that most journalists have in clearly defining their professional product.
18. Paletz and Entman, *Media Power Politics*, p. 17.
19. Robert Darnton, "Writing News and Telling Stories," *Daedalus* 104 (Spring 1975): 190.
20. Lewis H. Lapham, "Gilding the News," *Harper's*, July 1981, p. 34.
21. Ibid.
22. Paletz and Entman, *Media Power Politics*, p. 16.
23. Reported in Barrett, "Folksy TV News," p. 19.
24. I am indebted to Liz McHale for bringing this phenomenon to my attention.
25. Tuchman, *Making News*, chap. 1.
26. Lapham, *Gilding the News*, p. 35.
27. Opening paragraph of a column by Laura Cunningham, *New York Times*, 3 September 1981, Home Section, p. 16.
28. Russell Baker, "Meanwhile, in Zanzibar ...," *New York Times Magazine*, 6 February 1977, p. 12.
29. Edwin Diamond, "Disco News," in *Watching American Politics*, ed., Dan Nimmo and William L. Rivers (New York: Longman, 1981), p. 250.
30. Paletz and Entman, *Media Power Politics*, p. 23.
31. See the *Wall Street Journal*, 30 April, 5 May, 11 May, 3 June, and 17 June 1981.
32. See, for example, Edward Jay Epstein's fascinating suggestion that there may have been a much larger scandal behind Watergate than the one revealed in the story of "all the President's men." The dramatic plot helped confine the story to the White House. Moreover, any suggestion of larger conspiracies involved would have overburdened the already complex plot and undermined the credibility of the neatly contained White House story. See Edward Jay Epstein, "The Grand Coverup," *Wall Street Journal*, 19 April 1976, p. 10.
33. For detailed discussions of these findings, see W. Lance Bennett, *The Political Mind and the Political Environment: An Investigation of Public Opinion and Political Consciousness* (Lexington, Mass.: Heath, 1975); and Bennett, *Public Opinion in American Politics* (New York: Harcourt Brace Jovanovich, 1980).
34. CBS Radio Network News, 11 p.m. Eastern Time, 16 September 1981.
35. For further evidence and analysis of these patterns in reporting, see Edie Goldenberg, *Making the Papers* (Lexington, Mass.: Heath-Lexington Books, 1975); and Gitlin, *The Whole World Is Watching*.
36. For various explanations of this tendency, see, among others, Epstein, *News from Nowhere*; Crouse, *The Boys on the Bus*; Sigal, *Reporters and Officials*; Gitlin, *The Whole World Is Watching*; Tuchman, *Making News*; and Gans, *Deciding What's News*.
37. Sanford J. Ungar, "North and South at the Summit," *Atlantic*, January 1982, p. 7.
38. C. Jack Orr, "Reporters Confront the President: Sustaining a Counterpoised Situation." *Quarterly Journal of Speech* 66 (February 1980): 17–32.

39. See W. Lance Bennett, "Assessing Presidential Character: Degradation Rituals in Presidential Campaigns," *Quarterly Journal of Speech* 67 (October 1981): 310–21.
40. NBC News "White Paper" on the Reagan Presidency, 10 p.m. Pacific Time Zone, 30 December 1981.
41. A case described by Epstein in *News from Nowhere*.
42. See virtually any mass media news story during 1981 on the topic of the Polish unions.
43. Margaret Yao, "Under Deng's Regime, Urban Chinese Families Feather Their Nests," *Wall Street Journal*, 8 September 1981, p. 18.
44. For a more detailed explanation of how this sort of political reasoning persists, see W. Lance Bennett, "Myth, Ritual, and Political Control," *Journal of Communication* 30 (Autumn 1980): 166–79.
45. Lapham, "Gilding the News," p. 33.
46. Tuchman, *Making News*, p. 87.

TWO

How Politicians Make the News

> ... when information which properly belongs to the public is withheld by those in power, the people soon become ignorant of their own affairs, distrustful of those who manage them, and—eventually—incapable of determining their own destinies.
>
> RICHARD NIXON

At the close of World War II, the victorious Allied Powers met to divide Europe into spheres of influence. These meetings—between Churchill and Stalin at Moscow in 1944 and between Roosevelt, Churchill, and Stalin at Yalta in 1945—were proclaimed in public to be reasoned deliberations that would ensure peace, stability, and freedom in the world for all time. Following Yalta, Roosevelt pointed to the Soviet promise of free elections in Poland as an example of the commitment to democracy that prevailed at the meeting. Stalin echoed Roosevelt's claim with the public assurance that "Poland must be free, independent, and powerful."

In contrast to these lofty images of the meetings and their results, another reality prevailed behind the closed doors of Moscow and Yalta. The agreement at Yalta excluded the Polish government in exile from a serious role in forming the new government. With this agreement, the three heads of state knew that there would be no real "freedom" in the elections that would be held two years later. In fact, their decision paved the way for the tradition of Soviet domination in Poland that persists to this day.

Churchill's own account of the Moscow session revealed that an atmosphere of brute political bargaining guided the division of the Balkan states. A half sheet of paper was used to jot down the amounts of "influence" the victors would exert in the territories in question: Romania, 90 percent Russian influence; Greece, 90 percent British; Yugoslavia and Hungary, a 50–50 split; Bulgaria, 75 percent for Russia. Following the bargaining, Churchill gave the paper to Stalin for his approval. According to Churchill's own account, Stalin simply "took his blue pencil and made a large tick upon it." Whereupon Churchill asked: "Might it not be thought rather cynical if it seemed we had disposed of these issues, so fateful to millions of people, in such an off-hand manner?" He proposed burning the paper, but Stalin insisted that Churchill keep it.[1]

There are two realities in the above story. One involves the actual political behaviors and concerns of powerful actors. The other involves the cosmetic presentation of a newsworthy version of the event, a version inspired by concerns about how the actual circumstances might "seem" to the public. Political actors are confronted constantly with concerns about how the actual politics of an event might "seem" and whether a more "seemly" image can be created and used to some political advantage.

Leaders who disillusion their followers live shorter political lives than leaders who learn to re-present situations to their best political advantage. It is hardly surprising, therefore, that the news is filled with self-interested, timeworn, romanticized, and often irrelevant versions of events. It is often argued (usually by retired politicians) that the practice of deception is the only recourse, given the unpleasant realities of politics. Despite this common lament of the poor politician, one suspects that the realities of politics would not be so unpleasant if leaders were more serious about representing the interests and ideals of their followers. It is unfortunate that the selfless representation of others' interests is so seldom the stuff of which power is made or places in history won. Even more unfortunate, for those of us who watch world events from the outside, is the fact that it is almost never possible to know how closely the public version of an event conforms to the actual political circumstances involved. Indeed, the mark of skill in the political trade is the ability to make the public version of a situation convincing, no matter how far removed from actuality it may be. As former Secretary of State Dean Acheson once said, the task of public officers seeking support for their policies is to make their points "clearer than truth."[2]

On occasion, the contrived aspects of news stories are exposed as a result of slips, blunders, leaks, miscalculations, or defections of former insiders. For example, when Gerald Ford pardoned Richard Nixon for his Watergate crimes, Ford lost favor with many Americans who began to suspect ulterior motives in his earlier, "altruistic" proposal of amnesty for Vietnam draft resisters.[3] When the U.S.-backed attempt to overthrow the Castro regime in Cuba ended in a military disaster at the Bay of Pigs in 1961, the Kennedy administration could no longer use the planned cover story that the invasion force of Cuban exiles (with its captured American equipment) had acted independently of the U.S. government.[4] President Eisenhower's repeated denials of U.S. spy flights over the Soviet Union became embarrassingly transparent with the Russian capture of a U-2 spy plane on the eve of a major summit conference.[5] Ronald Reagan's economic explanations lost some of their luster when David Stockman, budget director and chief interpreter of "Reaganomics," disclosed that economic figures had been "adjusted" to fit Reagan's "supply side" economic models.[6]

Perhaps because it occurs so rarely, it is exciting, dramatic, and somehow satisfying when a political cover drops to reveal a darker reality of corruption, power, and deceit. It is hard to forget the ending of the Watergate scandal when news correspondents led the country in the near-universal cheer, "The System Worked!" It is ironic that such conclusions often accompany revelations of political deception. In the specific case of Watergate, the "system" pardoned the worst offender, gave light sentences to most of the others, and made archvillians into media celebrities and millionaires in the process. Even when viewed in a less petty way, it is puzzling how an occasional revelation like Watergate can be used to exonerate "the system." History suggests that for every revelation on the order of Watergate, many more lie undetected until long after their political effects have been recorded.

History tells us, for example, that Lyndon Johnson's justification for large-scale American involvement in Vietnam was based on a largely fabricated account of "unprovoked" attacks on U.S. ships in the Gulf of Tonkin.[7] Johnson, like Roosevelt twenty-five years before him, had searched for an "incident" that would justify entry into a war. Perhaps it was cruel fate that history made a hero of Roosevelt by providing him an immaculate justification in the form of the Japanese attack on Pearl Harbor, while Johnson was forced to resort to the tawdry business of fabricating his own incident. History also tells us of the major role of the U.S. Central Intelligence Agency in the 1973 overthrow of the government of Chile. We even learned, many years after the fact, that the Kennedy administration authorized the overthrow of the South Vietnamese government in the early days of U.S. involvement in Vietnam. This revelation took a rather perverse path to historical disclosure. Feeling that he was both misunderstood and victimized by history, Lyndon Johnson resented being blamed for the "credibility gap" that undermined public support for his policies in Vietnam. Perhaps in an effort to show that even the glorified Kennedy administration was guilty of a credibility gap, Johnson leaked to a reporter copies of diplomatic cables linking President Kennedy to the assassination of President Diem and the overthrow of his regime.[8]

As these and other examples indicate, many cases of political deception are brought eventually to our attention through historical research, government investigation, or the release of secret documents. However, even if all past cases of news distortion were revealed after the fact (and this surely is not the case), such disclosure would not alter the political effects of the lying and deception prior to their discovery. The problem with political deception passing as news is that as long as it goes undetected and unchallenged, it *is* the political reality under which people live. As Walter Lippmann observed sixty years ago in his classic work on public opinion, "the only feeling that anyone can have about an event he does not experience is the feeling aroused by his mental image of that event."[9] There is very little check on the kinds of images that can be created for political situations when the information received by the masses of people on the outside of politics is controlled by a few people on the inside. As Secretary of State Acheson reminded us, the effective public official does not attempt to educate or convey "objective" images; the official's goal is to represent issues and events in ways that gain support, shape action, and influence outcomes.[10]

The fact that political actors make a practice of creating images for political situations does not mean that the news is filled with wild, diverse, and highly imaginative political stories. Unusual stories tend to appear when, as in the rare case of Watergate, the actual details of an event become known. To the contrary, most political images are based on familiar symbols, formula plots, standard slogans, and tired rhetoric.[11] As pointed out in the last chapter, the world of political images is built from predictable symbolic transformations: the new into the old, the startling into the familiar, the self-interested into the public spirited. Even threats and crises become presented in stereotypes of Soviet aggression, American firmness, "peace through strength," "productive and serious discussions," and so on.

There are those who argue that the news bias in favor of official, normalized political messages is not a bias at all; mainstream views should receive a lion's share of news attention precisely because they represent the center of political thinking in America. This argument clearly fails to consider the role of the news in creating and legitimizing "official" or "normal" politics in the first place. Even more important, the failure to regard normalized news as politically biased ignores the possibility that many official pronouncements are inaccurate and inadequate descriptions of real events. The lessons of history tell us that it is precisely through the repeated use of normalized political images that the greatest political deception and distortion occurs. Thus, a hidden problem with reporting "official positions" as the main news of the day is the resulting likelihood of communicating a considerable amount of deception, lying, and political fabrication disguised as fact.

There is, therefore, a profound irony in newsmaking. The credibility of a political image lies not in some independent check on its accuracy but in its past success as a news formula. *In this world of media reality, news-*

worthiness becomes a substitute for validity, and credibility becomes re-
duced to a formula of who applies what images to which events under what
circumstances. Ordinary logic tells us that the more standardized an image, the less valid and meaningful is its application to unique, real-world
situations. Media logic, on the other hand, tells us that reality *is* the image applied to it. The more "official" the position, the more likely it is to be
reported, and the more it is reported the more credibility it gains, and
the more credibility it gains, the more "official" it becomes. It is obvious why
common sense fares poorly in direct competition against media logic.
Like any successful logic, media logic is functional; it enables both news
and politics to operate on a routine, symbiotic basis. Common sense, by
comparison, is of little use in unraveling the news web of political secrecy,
double talk, and untestable abstraction.

If the images contained in official political positions were mere entertainment fare floating about in the electronic ether, there might be less
cause for concern (other than for the low quality of the plots that politicians foist upon their audiences). As long as the images in the news are
treated as real, however, people may be inclined to respond to them.
Even, and perhaps especially, those images with the most dubious links to
reality can generate actions in the real world, actions that have real
effects. The images planted in the news can result in the election of leaders, the acceptance of oppressive laws or ideas, the labeling of social
groups, support for wars, or tolerance of chronic social and economic
problems.

Who is to say that the Russians are really as hostile and deceitful as our
leaders have made them out to be for the last thirty years? Or that we are
as well intentioned, peaceable, and pure as our public relations doctrines
imply? When viewed apart from political images, both superpowers seem
to act in very similar ways in the world: supporting corrupt regimes,
building spheres of influence, tolerating human oppression, pursuing economic advantage, and alternating between postures of reconciliation and
aggression whenever it suits their purposes to do so. The images that each
side attaches to these behaviors are quite different, however. One side's
aggressive behavior evokes the other's defensive posture. Such has been
the enduring historical script for "moral" war and "justifiable" human
destruction. Thus the news images of the political world can be tragically
self-fulfilling. Dominant political images can create a world in their own
image—even when such a world did not exist to begin with.

The Goals of Image Making

In view of their political uses, it is not surprising that images are of great
concern to politicians. Failure to control the news is often equated with

political failure. As the campaign manager for a presidential candidate put it, "the media *is* the campaign."[12] Or, as a key presidential adviser implied, there is no political reality apart from news reality. That impression was conveyed by Ronald Reagan's top aide, James Baker, who was asked by an NBC correspondent why the President seemed so unwilling to compromise on a tough budget proposal he submitted to Congress. Baker said that any show of compromise or weakness was undesirable because, in the media, "everything is cast in terms of winning or losing."[13] Thus the President could not back down no matter how unrealistic his position. To be seen as unrealistic was preferable to being perceived as a loser, because being perceived as a loser would make him a loser.

It is clear that controlling political images in the news is a primary goal of politics, and, as such, it is important to understand what this entails. Most public relations experts agree that successful image making involves three things:

1. Composing a simple theme or message for the audience to use in thinking about the matter at hand. Call this *message composition*.
2. Saturating communications channels with this message so that it will become more salient than competing messages. Call this *message salience*.
3. Surrounding the message with the trappings of credibility so that, if it reaches people, it will be accepted. Call this *message credibility*.

Although these three components of political image making work together in actual political communication, it is useful to consider them separately in order to see what each one contributes to the audience's perception of a political situation.

Message Composition

The content of a political message is usually simple, familiar, and idealistic. Political messages generally begin with a key phrase, idea, or theme that creates a convenient way for people to think about a political object— be it an issue, an event, or even a person. For example, Franklin Roosevelt appealed to the hopes of the masses by using the simple term "the New Deal" to refer to his complex patchwork of untried economic programs. Borrowing these characteristics of simplicity and idealism, John Kennedy added the power of familiarity when he presented his programs to the people under the title of "the New Frontier." Ronald Reagan showed how far political connotations can be stretched by giving the simple, familiar, and idealistic name "the New Federalism" to his efforts to dismantle Roosevelt's "New Deal," Kennedy's "New Frontier," and Johnson's "Great Society."

Political themes and slogans can get an image started by encouraging people to imagine things about a situation. As the name implies, an image is not some concrete entity that exists "out there" in the world; it is the product of human imagination shaped by the suggestive symbolism of political messages. The symbolic component of an image is so simplistic, abstract, and free of detail that the only way it can make sense is for people to add their own interpretations, fantasies, and concerns. *Thus an image is an impression of something that is anchored partly in a symbolic suggestion and partly in the feelings and assumptions that people have in response to that suggestion.* When people begin to supply the facts and feelings necessary to complete an image, the symbolic "message" component of political communication seems increasingly real and convincing; hence, the irony that from some of the most simplistic and insubstantial ideas emerge some of the most heartfelt understandings.

When Richard Nixon's campaign strategists assessed his presidential prospects in 1968, they concluded that the biggest problem was the widespread perception that he was a "loser." In response to this problem the campaign was launched with the symbolic suggestion that there was a "new Nixon." Such an idea was every bit as illusory as the careful scripting of Nixon's new character. As with many effective political themes, however, the "new Nixon" became a much-discussed term that created for many people a seemingly concrete and legitimate reference for political actions that otherwise might have been seen as ambiguous or deceitful.[14]

Message Salience

Creating an image requires more than inventing a catchy theme or slogan. Images come into being only when the symbolic component, or message, becomes a frequent point of departure for the popular imagination. Lots of catchy messages elude popular imagination because they fail to capture widespread attention. The need for a message to capture attention explains why the second goal of image making is to saturate communication channels with the message. If a message becomes more prominent than its competition, it stands a greater chance of shaping public thought and action. The goal of message salience explains why advertisers spend billions of dollars to chant their simple jingles and slogans over and over again in the media. The same goal explains why politicians spend considerable energy trying to get their simplistic messages incorporated in the plots of news stories.

It is not always easy for political actors to make their messages salient. Even though the salient messages in most news stories come from official sources, there is no guarantee that any particular official source can get its message across at will. In fact, recent political history suggests that many powerful figures end up the victims of the same news media that helped create them in the first place. Journalists can exercise many reporting options that may undermine the salience of a political message. The most obvious option is that reporters can simply stop covering an actor who, in their estimation, is no longer able to present a message in dramatic or effective ways. Alternatively, reporters can reduce the strength of an actor's political "signal" by boosting the coverage given to opponents' messages. In some rare cases, reporters may even undermine message salience by exposing a politician's claims for what they really are, namely, transparent symbols with little real substance. These last two reporting options are particularly nasty because they damage credibility at the same time that they reduce salience. Such are the perils of life in the symbol business; today's truth may become tomorrow's travesty.

Boosting the salience of a message that is on the upswing makes the news media seem to be harbingers of new and creative ideas, while undermining the salience of stale messages makes journalists appear to be defenders of truth and political competition. However, it is worth recognizing that most of the messages eventually undermined by the media were promoted by them in the first place. Moreover, a message that loses salience in the news generally does so because another equally illusory symbolic creation takes its place. Perhaps most important, the real political effects of messages during their periods of news salience may be irreversible by the time they become deemphasized.

Although media decisions about what to emphasize and deemphasize in the news often seem arbitrary or capricious, there do appear to be patterns involved. For example, Paletz and Entman discovered three conditions surrounding the Presidency that seem to affect whether the media will pass along a President's messages without commentary or whether they will dilute message salience with critical commentary or opposing views.[15] The first condition involves the "media status" of the President. If he is early in his term and effective in projecting a strong media image, the news is more likely to give strong emphasis to his chosen messages. Second, the more solemn the occasion or the more important the issue, the more undivided attention his messages will receive. Finally, the greater the perceived elite and public support the President has, the more salient his messages will be. Or, as Paletz and Entman put this last point, "the greater the opposition is believed to be, the more emboldened network correspondents are in their analysis."[16]

Paletz and Entman illustrate these conditions with the example of a news conference held by Richard Nixon during the darkest days of his Watergate crisis. Understanding the requirements of symbolic composition, Nixon chose a setting, an audience, and a set of carefully prepared messages designed to convey the impressions that he was far removed from Watergate and that the Watergate affair paled with insignificance by comparison to his other accomplishments in office. Following the conference, however, was an "instant analysis" session in which CBS news correspondent Roger Mudd said: "I cannot see an awful lot of news in tonight's broadcast. . . ."[17] Mudd and his colleagues then went on to remark about the handpicked audience and the political motives behind the messages that Nixon took such pains to deliver during the conference. Did such commentary have an effect on the salience of Nixon's messages? In order to assess this question, Paletz and Entman showed a tape of the news conference only to a group of people who had not witnessed the original performance. A tape of the conference plus the instant analysis was shown to another group in the experiment. The group who did not see the instant analysis emerged much more supportive of the President and his views.[18]

In view of the above findings, it is not hard to understand why politicians are so concerned with their images. In a sense, they are right in thinking that image is everything. Images feed on each other. To the extent that politicians can create appealing leadership images, salience is more likely to be conferred on their specific political pronouncements. To the extent that issues can be made to seem important by calling them crises or associating them with high symbols of state, opposing voices are more likely to be drowned out. To the extent that public favor can be won, future messages will receive less criticism, thereby escalating the spiral of popularity, thereby increasing future message salience, and so on. Politicians who create such networks of reinforcing images are likely to be more successful in attaining the goal of message salience.

Message Credibility

Even a public bombarded with salient political messages cannot always be relied on to accept them. Only in the advanced stages of becoming media zombies can people be expected to believe everything they hear. Salient political messages are more likely to be supported when they are accompanied by some measure of their validity. Common sense tells us that arguments are more credible when they include sound logic, solid evidence, or reference to authorities. Most political images make some use of logic, evidence, or authoritative endorsement.

Unfortunately, common sense may fail us in our efforts to distinguish reliable trappings of credibility from unreliable or irrelevant ones. For example, when the Defense Department defends its budget requests every year, it plays a game requiring considerable symbolic skill. On the one hand, the testimony must reassure Congress and the people that the huge amounts spent on defense in the past have paid off in terms of American strength and preparedness. This calls for the introduction of facts and expert testimony to support an image of strength. On the other hand, the Defense Department must show that without continued and even greater expenditures, the United States will fall hopelessly behind in the arms race. This calls for impressive charts and graphs showing impending losses in weapon strength and technological sophistication. Enter an image of weakness.

If this image game is played well, the supporting evidence presented by the nation's most credible experts will lead to a logical conclusion every time: If the government will only fund the new arms programs proposed this year, the gap between the frightening image of weakness and the reassuring image of strength can be closed. At least until next year when the statistics are brought out anew, the experts appear again, defense logic fills the hearing rooms, and as if by magic, the image of America as a cowering helpless giant once again appears in the minds of Americans.

It is impossible to know, of course, whether the experts and their figures are right because we have not had the chance to test their logic in a real nuclear war. But the trappings of credibility need not have anything to do with reality. They are instrumental in creating an image. The image is so terrifying that we are led to hope that by giving the defense officials what they want it will go away. And as if by magic, it does go away every year. In the process, we reinforce the very trappings of credibility that will bring it back again next year. How? By granting expenditures for arms programs in order to make the image of weakness disappear, we legitimize the use of the same "logic," "evidence," and "authorities" the next time that the image of weakness is released, like a genie, from the generals' briefcases.

The Techniques of Image Making

The goals of image making are fairly straightforward: Select a theme or message to spark the imagination; make sure that the chosen message dominates communication about the matter at hand; and surround the message with the trappings of credibility. Simple though they may appear, attaining these goals is no easy matter. Effective image making requires sophisticated understanding and use of various communication techniques. There is, of course, no lack of time, energy, resources, or personnel devoted to the deployment of image techniques. For example, it has been estimated that anywhere from 30 to 50 percent of the large and well-paid White House staff is involved with media relations in some form.[19] It has been argued that the major preoccupation of the average member of the House of Representatives is running for the next election.[20] The Defense Department spends billions of dollars annually from its huge budget on public relations of one sort or another.[21] The U.S. Army even runs a special school to train its corps of public relations officers.[22] In view of these efforts, one observer has concluded that "the vast, interlocking federal information machine has one primary purpose: the selling of the government."[23] What do the public relations experts do? To put it simply, they use symbols in ways calculated to best satisfy the goals of image making.

Symbols

Symbols are the basic units of most human communication. Words are symbols that stand for objects and ideas. Flags, emblems, and uniforms are symbols of nationalism, group, or authority. Specific people can even symbolize general human attributes like heroism, patriotism, beauty, or greed. As these examples suggest, symbols stand for, or represent, things (objects, places, ideas, etc.) for purposes of communication about those things. Because of the existence of symbols, it is possible to communicate about something without having the object of communication immediately present. Thus, the word "tree" is a symbol that permits communication about trees whether or not a tree is present in the situation. The term "nuclear war" permits communication about something that does not exist anywhere except in the frailty of the human imagination.

Symbols permit the recounting and vicarious sharing of experiences with people who did not participate in those experiences firsthand. Because of symbols, complex ideas and messages can be transmitted simply— as when the appearance of a uniformed police officer conveys a large set of understandings to people at the scene of a crime. Much of the routine business of life (including, unfortunately, subjects in the news) can be reduced to symbolic formulas for purposes of efficient communication. Symbols even permit our imaginations to work in concert to create and share ideas about things that have never existed (a unicorn) and things that may one day exist (a genetically engineered unicorn clone).

Since a major preoccupation of politicians is how to represent actual situations in the most favorable terms possible, it is obvious why symbols are so important in politics. Through the skillful use of symbols, actual political circumstances can be redefined and, for all practical purposes, replaced with a wide range of alternative references. In short, symbols offer politicians strategic choices about how to engage the popular imagination in any political situation.

In order to understand how symbols are used and what makes them effective or ineffective, it is useful to know something about their psychological effects. Every symbol has at least two effects on us. One effect engages our thinking processes. This *cognitive* effect is responsible for the basic meaning of a symbolic message. The second effect engages our emotions, or *affect*, by triggering a feeling about the message. The cognitive effect involves the possible meanings for any symbol, which can be narrow and specific or can be broad and numerous. For example, the term "freedom" has multiple associations for nearly everyone. In contrast, the term "congressional delegation" has a narrow, specific meaning. On the affective side, a symbol may elicit little emotional response or may evoke great outpourings of feeling. For example, the term "freedom" can be used in highly emotional ways, while "congressional delegation" provokes relatively little emotion from most people under most circumstances. Symbols that convey narrow meaning with little emotion are called *referential symbols*. Symbols that evoke broad categories of meaning accompanied by strong emotions are called *condensational symbols*.[24] We have even invented symbols to help us talk about symbols!

The kind of image created for a political situation depends on what the key actors want the public to do in the situation. A faction interested in broadening the scope and intensity of public involvement may picture a situation in condensational symbols, while a faction interested in narrowing the scope and intensity of public concern can be expected to use referential terms. For example, groups that opposed U.S. actions in Vietnam represented the bombing of North Vietnam in condensational terms emphasizing savage destruction, government lying, and dangerous expansion of the war. The government, on the other hand, sought to minimize public concern with the details of the war. Public relations officers in the White House and the Pentagon invented an entire vocabulary of referential symbols to blunt the meanings and feelings attached to military actions. Thus, bombing raids on North Vietnam were referred to as "protective reactions strikes"—a term so narrow and bloodless that only its creators understood precisely what it implied.

Whether a particular symbol has referential or condensational effects depends partly on the symbol and partly on how it is used. In the right context, even the most innocuous referential term can be transformed into a powerful condensational symbol. For example, in the early days of the Vietnam war the Pentagon used the term "missing in action" (MIA for short) to refer to the number of troops missing and unaccounted for in combat. For years, this symbol was a descriptive term with a specific meaning and little emotional charge. Over the years, however, the number of MIAs grew, and many Americans became increasingly upset about the failure of anyone to account for these sons, friends, husbands, and lovers. Also during this time, the country became polarized into pro- and anti-war factions, making for a highly charged emotional atmosphere. In the middle of this situation was Richard Nixon, who searched for some effective way of justifying his continued war policies despite broad opposition to them. Suddenly Nixon had his issue. He explained to the public that the breakdowns in his peace negotiations had been due largely to the refusal of the North Vietnamese to promise an accounting of prisoners of war and MIAs. He told the public that he could not end the war and turn his back on those brave soldiers. Seemingly from out of nowhere came demonstrations and endorsement of his position. Bumper stickers proclaiming the plight of the MIAs appeared everywhere. In the space of a few months the symbol had acquired a new way of being used, and the change of usage transformed it from an obscure referential term to a powerful condensational symbol. The lesson is important: *Symbols are not static; their communicational effects (both meanings and emotional impact) depend in large part on how they are used in specific contexts.*

This dynamic quality of symbolism helps explain why the narrow, redundant messages of "officialized" politics do not become intolerable to people. Since there are numerous ways to refer to almost anything, and since the real world constantly provides new contexts in which to place messages, there is a constant potential for subtle variation in the form or style of political communication. Cross-cultural studies of art, music, humor, literature, drama, architecture, folk tales, and, increasingly, political communication support the observation that human (and most other) intelligence is programmed to respond to variations on familiar patterns. People are attracted both cognitively and affectively to new twists on, or new contexts for, old themes.

In the case of politics, unfortunately, the old themes to which people respond are often poor representations of reality. To some extent the poverty of political representation is disguised by the distance of political events from people's lives, combined with the intimacy and immediacy with which those events are represented by symbols in the news. Moreover, since people are creatures that seek meaning in their lives, the domination of political communication by a narrow range of political meaning encourages many people to accept official messages rather than settle for the doubt, anxiety, and social pressures associated with the search for meaning outside mainstream channels of information.

The news, of course, magnifies all the factors affecting the acceptance of normalized political messages. First, by emphasizing style over content, the news exaggerates the drama and distinctiveness of old messages when such messages are presented with new scripts or new contexts. Second, by reporting dramatized and stylized political performances as though they represented the real motives and issues at stake in political situations, the news promotes the acceptance of often distorted symbolic versions of events. Finally, by implicitly endorsing official views and closing off the presentation of alternative information, the news enhances the psychological appeal of official meaning while undermining the appeal of alternative perspectives.

Although the flexibility of symbols is a great resource for transforming the real world of politics into a world of "realistic" political images, this flexibility also contains a hidden danger for politicians. So great are the possible gaps between symbol and reality that actors sometimes lose their sense of what will "play in Peoria" and propose truly absurd or transparent definitions of situations. For example, a local police department's increase in radar patrol activity triggered angry citizen protests against that spine-chilling condensational symbol "speed trap." The department launched a public relations effort to cool off the citizens with the reassurance that the radar activities were no more than "accident prevention patrols" and that worried motorists could call a special number to find out where these patrols were located each day (presumably so that the motorists would be sure to avoid having accidents in those areas).[25] In another case, the owners of a nuclear power plant that leaked radioactive gas were determined not to let the incident become a major news story like the one that haunted the nuclear power industry following the 1979 leak at Three Mile Island, Pennsylvania. The leak at the Louisa, Virginia, plant was followed by an eleven-hour communication blackout during which time press briefings were scripted for simultaneous delivery at the plant site and at the Nuclear Regulatory Commission headquarters in Washington, D.C. The opening announcement stated that the plant "burped" a small amount of radioactive gas into the atmosphere. To clarify this idea, the company spokesperson said, "It wasn't a leak, it was more like a burp."[26] In this case, the choice of a ridiculous metaphor evidently did no harm, as the story died quickly.

Many political problems cannot be dismissed simply by turning speed traps into accident prevention patrols or nuclear gas leaks into burps. Some problems have widely recognized names, and the challenge for the public official becomes more a matter of avoiding their use than inventing a transparent substitute. For example, when unemployment goes up and productivity and profits go down, and the pattern persists, most people agree that the country is in a "recession." This condensational symbol strikes fear in the hearts of everyone—brokers, bankers, investors, workers, and, above all, Presidents, who are blamed for the situation. Most Presidents faced with recessions engage in an amusing dance to avoid the use of the term, even when the situation is clearly defined. In one of the more blatant efforts to dodge the recession symbol, a Nixon administration press secretary fielded the following reporter's question at a time when the country had experienced several months of the dreaded word:

Q: How long do you expect the recession to last?
A: Well, it won't last long at all because we don't consider it a recession.
Q: How's that?
A: Well, we don't want to view the current economic situation as a recession. Therefore, it can't last very long.
Q: But what do you call the current situation?
A: It is from our standpoint a perfectly normal fluctuation in the economic cycle. You see, the term recession is very political. Our opposition would love to pin it on us, and we, of course, would rather not be stuck with it. So, unless something really disastrous happens, we won't talk about recession.[27]

Some years later, Ronald Reagan confronted another recession, one that he promised to prevent if elected President. After first denying it and then avoiding it, he finally acknowledged the situation in the most casual possible way. As he was leaving the White House on his way to meet a visiting dignitary, Reagan casually remarked to a reporter: "I think there's a slight and I hope a short recession. I think everyone agrees on that."[28]

From Symbol to News

When a simple message is used as a caption for a complex issue or event, the first step has been taken toward creating an image. As suggested earlier, however, simply throwing symbols at a situation does not guarantee that the popular imagination will be engaged by them. Even more important than the symbols is their presentation to the news media. The salience, credibility, and image effects of political symbols depend on whether the ways they are presented to reporters make them the basis for news reports about the situation.

In some cases there is very little that a political actor can do to turn a political message into a widely reported news story. For example, when Jimmy Carter urged the country to "wage the moral equivalent of war" against its energy problems, the phrase was reported more widely as a sign of Carter's desperation than as a valid description of the magnitude of the energy problem. Carter had violated the three canons of journalistic respect: He was a faltering President, with low popular and elite support, speaking on an issue that at the time was not regarded as serious by a majority of the public.

When conditions are better suited to journalistic cooperation, public officials often succeed in dictating the content of news stories. Public officials have the resources to script and stage well-produced political performances. Most high officials have writers, media directors, costume consultants, readily available dramatic settings, and an attentive press corps ready to cover official announcements and events. Through the careful preparation of messages, public officials often succeed in controlling the information pertaining to all the key elements of the news story: the *scene*, the status of the *actor*, the motives or *"ends"* the political action is to serve, the *"means"* through which the action will accomplish its ends, and the significance of the political *action* itself. The goal, of course, is to control information pertaining to all the components of the unfolding "real-life political drama," and thereby control the content of the news stories written about the situation. However, some situations are too spontaneous, and some actors too poor in skills or resources, to control all news information about an event. Thus, attempts at the political manipulation of the news run along a continuum from fully controlled news events at one end, to partially controlled news events in the middle, to uncontrolled events at the other extreme.

Fully Controlled News

Fully controlled media presentations are often called *"pseudoevents."*[29] Pseudoevents disguise actual political circumstances with "realistic" representations designed to create politically useful images. A pseudoevent uses careful stage setting, scripting, and acting to create convincing images that often have little to do with the underlying reality of the situation. By incorporating only fragments of an actual situation into a dramatized presentation, a pseudoevent tempts the imagination to build a complete understanding out of fragmentary facts. In a well-fashioned pseudoevent, the script, the action, and the setting make enough reference to known properties of the situation to cause difficulty in distinguishing between what is real and what is merely "realistic."

The distinction between real and realistic is illustrated by a pseudoevent used by Richard Nixon to shape public reaction to a disastrous oil spill in the Santa Barbara Channel in 1969. Nixon intervened in the situation because the environmental issues involved had become added to the growing list of concerns being addressed by the volatile antigovernment student movement. Using his status and popularity as a newly elected President, Nixon quickly intervened in the situation to create the impression that the oil spill was no longer a major problem and that the damage had been repaired. After announcing that the situation had been serious but was now under control, Nixon completed the pseudoevent by conducting an "inspection tour" of a sparkling clean Santa Barbara beach. This walk on the beach would have been less convincing had he (or the press) announced that the chosen stretch of beach had been cleaned especially for the event, while miles of beach to the north and south "remained hopelessly blackened."[30]

The Nixon walk on the beach displayed the defining properties of most of the pseudoevents that dominate the daily news. According to Boorstin's definition, a pseudoevent has four characteristics:

1. It is not spontaneous, but comes about because someone has planned, planted, or incited it.
2. It is planted primarily for the immediate purpose of being reported.
3. Its relation to the underlying reality of the situation is ambiguous.
4. It is intended to be self-fulfilling.[31]

Both the trip to Santa Barbara and the walk on a prepared beach were planned for purposes of being reported as news (points 1 and 2 above). Indeed, the event contained the makings of a great news story: A new President visits the visually interesting scene of a dramatic disaster to show his concern for the problem. The relation between the news story and the underlying reality of the situation was ambiguous (point 3) in the sense that the image of reassurance and concern disguised a reality of devastation and cynical lack of care. The public was shown a real beach; it just was not shown the real problem. Finally, the event was self-fulfilling (point 4). The news created the image that the problem had been solved because the media reported an event in which the problem seemed to be solved. In the world of politics, it is often easier to create the appearance that a problem has been solved than to solve it.

How effective are pseudoevents in shaping the news? A well-conceived event has such strong story lines that it becomes hard for reporters to find alternative news angles. Even when truly significant spontaneous occurrences find their way by accident into a carefully staged performance, the overall theme of the performance is often strong enough to downplay the spontaneous elements in the plots of resulting news stories. In 1970, for example, Richard Nixon shared his Thanksgiving dinner with a group of wounded Vietnam veterans. The event served the dual purpose of counteracting his image as a "cold" person and promoting support for his new interest in the human side of the war (i.e., the fates of missing, captured, and wounded troops). Even though many of the invited soldiers decided to spend the day with families, the empty places in the White House dining room were filled with staff members from the local Naval hospital. On cue, the press was ushered in for a brief picture session. After the dinner, an enterprising reporter decided to interview the soldiers who sat at Nixon's table. During these interviews the reporter discovered the bombshell news that Nixon had mentioned a daring attempt to rescue American prisoners from a North Vietnamese POW camp. This disclosure was big news on several accounts. First, the raid involved an offensive mission into North Vietnam, risking a possible escalation of the war during a period of intense peace efforts. Second, the secretary of defense and other officers of the administration had lied repeatedly under oath during congressional testimony, claiming that no such raids had taken place. Finally, the raid had been a failure, indicating possible breakdowns in U.S. intelligence and special forces capabilities. Despite the importance of these factors, the reporter and his editors at the *Washington Post* decided to base the headline story on "the President spends Thanksgiving with the troops" angle. Nixon's disclosures were buried in later paragraphs of that article.[32]

Partially Controlled News

Some political situations are not as easy to control as Thanksgiving dinner with the troops or a walk on a beach. Many public settings have an element of spontaneity in them. For example, press conferences can be controlled insofar as choice of time, place, and opening remarks, but they always contain some risk of unexpected or hostile questions from the press. In other cases, an official may be surprised by an issue and asked to comment, even though he or she is unprepared to do so. When the comforting script of a pseudoevent is unavailable, political actors must resort to other means of protecting desired images.

A common means of handling partially controlled situations is to anticipate and prevent possible moments of spontaneity in advance. For example, press conferences are often structured tightly to promote desired messages and prevent spontaneous distractions. In a press conference, opening remarks can be written in newsworthy style, reporters can be called on or ignored, time limits can be imposed, and stage settings can be manipulated. Some officials grant interviews only if certain "ground rules" are agreed to by reporters. Some sensitive remarks may be branded as "off the record" and thereby censored from reporters' stories. Some actors limit their public appearances to avoid spontaneous settings, particularly those with reporters present.

In short, the struggle over partially controlled political turf is an ongoing one, with the victories generally going to high-status officials who can use prestige, power, and other resources (e.g., busy official schedules) to define their relations with the press. When those rare moments of spontaneous exchange do occur, the news most often records only those patented political avoidance terms like "no comment" or those windy bursts of political rhetoric that seem to have nothing to do with the issue at hand.

Sometimes the most effective means of operating in an uncontrolled situation is to hide in the background and release information via an anonymous news "leak." Leaks are useful for delivering messages in many unstable situations. In some cases an official may favor a policy but not know how the public will react. An anonymous leak describing the policy gives the official a chance to change course if the opposition is too strong. In other cases the information leaked is privileged or secret, thereby presenting problems for any kind of formal public release. At times, the political message is not important enough to guarantee coverage if released through normal press channels or presented as a pseudo-event. If the right reporter is given a "scoop" based on the information, however, the chances are pretty good that the story will receive special attention. Strong emphasis given to a story by one news outlet may prompt others to cover it the next day. This use of leaks was acknowledged humorously when Ronald Reagan opened a press conference by saying that he did not have an opening remark because his planned statement was so important that he decided to leak it instead, thereby boosting the chance that it would receive the media attention it deserved.

Sometimes leaks come in handy for repairing images damaged by news reports of opposing views. During the election of 1980, for example, Jimmy Carter pursued a "rose garden" campaign strategy. He staged numerous pseudoevents at the White House designed to show off the trappings of incumbency along with his deep involvement in solving the nation's problems. Since Carter was blessed with none of the conditions for favorable news coverage and since the news formulas pertaining to elections emphasize opposition attacks, Carter's desired image was taking a beating in the news. In response, the Carter staff leaked a memo from the President to his chief advisers explaining why the demands of office prevented his participation in the first of the televised debates between the candidates.[33] Such leaks can provide touches of "independent documentation" for faltering pseudoevents.

Leaks also offer control over one of the most important variables in partially controlled situations: timing. The timing of a leak or a press release is crucial. For example, it is common wisdom that bad news is best released on weekends when reporters are off duty, news programs are scarce, and the public is distracted from mundane concerns. In other cases, the issue of timing means getting the jump on opponents who may attempt to plant their own images about a situation. A well-timed leak may accomplish these and other goals of "timed release" information while disguising the motives of the actors involved. Such was the case with the Reagan administration's presentation of the 1983 budget. The proposed budget was a political disaster. There were huge deficits where Reagan had promised a balanced budget. There were painful cuts in already weakened social programs. To top it all off, the country was in serious economic trouble. The political task was to soften the blow of more bad news.

Normally the budget is delivered to the press on a Friday with a strict embargo not to publish any stories about it until after the President has delivered his budget message to Congress and the nation on Monday. The early release allows reporters to digest the huge mass of information in order to write stories around the President's message. The embargo ensures that the President's message will be the salient news theme at the start of the week. The Reagan media staff evidently decided that the budget was such a gross departure from Reagan's earlier promises that the news on Monday would be both salient and negative. To prevent this result, the budget director leaked the budget on Friday by "forgetting" his prepared materials in a congressional hearing room following a high-level congressional briefing. In a few hours the budget was in the hands of news people without the usual embargo. Since a summary of the President's message was included in the briefing materials, the story that would have dominated Monday's headlines was, instead, scattered across the less visible weekend news channels. By Monday, the news concentrated more on other angles than on damaging comparisons between what Reagan promised and what he delivered. When asked about the apparent leak, White House communication director David Gergen denied it and explained that the embargo stamp had been omitted "accidentally" from the budget books taken to the briefing.[34]

Uncontrolled News

Few things strike more fear in the heart of a politician than a news story that has gotten out of control. Sometimes control of a story is lost because the underlying reality of a situation is simply too big to hide, as was the case with Lyndon Johnson's increasingly empty assurances that the United States was winning the war in Vietnam. In some cases, former insiders "blow the cover" on a story, as happened when John Dean delivered his damaging Watergate testimony against Richard Nixon, or when former war strategist Daniel Ellsberg leaked secret government documents about Vietnam. In many instances, a story gets out of control when a

politician fails to handle the pressures of a partially controlled situation —
a classic case in point was Gerald Ford's blunder during a presidential
debate when he claimed there was no Soviet domination in Eastern
Europe. Sometimes the news slips from a politician's grasp simply because some problems cannot be solved or dismissed by the mere use of
self-fulfilling pseudoevents. For example, Ronald Reagan dominated the
news for over a year with his promise that "supply side" economics would
cure the nation's economic ills and balance the national budget. When
Reagan submitted a budget with a $150 billion deficit at the height of a
serious recession, the news became much more critical of his economic
pronouncements.

A typical pattern in loss of news control is for an actor to first generate
images successfully, only to eventually run afoul of leaks, blunders, or
uncontrollable events in the world. Few news stories are bigger than the
ones written about fallen political idols and struggling politicians. The
more the actor loses control over the situation, the bigger the story becomes. Reporters can be unmerciful in covering politicians who fail to
manipulate the news effectively. It is, as discussed in the last chapter,
easy to confuse news drama with political importance. Often the only real
impact of critical news coverage is on the personal image or career of the
actor. However, it is tempting to think that something significant is going
on because we have been conditioned to news that concentrates on personal political fortunes as though they were the major issues of our times.

Most politicians play right into the personal focus of the news because
they do take it personally when the news turns against them. Richard
Nixon left politics in 1962 with the bitter remark that the press would not
"have Nixon to kick around anymore." Lyndon Johnson called CBS president Frank Stanton frequently to harangue him about unfavorable news
coverage. In fact, many politicians become so concerned with favorable
news coverage that they go well beyond the use of conventional symbolic
techniques in their efforts to secure it. Some political actors even resort to
various kinds of intimidation tactics in their dealings with journalists.

It is common practice for politicians to monitor news coverage closely
and to adjust dealings with reporters according to the desirability of the
coverage. Stuart Loory, a reporter for the *Los Angeles Times*, recounted
an incident of intimidation that occurred when he was a member of the
press corps accompanying President Nixon on a European trip. Loory
noted that the pope gave Nixon a greeting at the Vatican that was unchar-
acteristically political in content. The pope hinted at criticisms of U.S. policies in the Middle East and Vietnam. Loory noted that the tone was
unusual in a public greeting, and wrote of the pope's "polite coolness"
toward Nixon. The very next day, in Yugoslavia, top presidential aide
H. R. Haldeman confronted Loory and demanded an accounting of the

article. Loory noted that "Haldeman had a report back on my story twenty-four hours later," even though the story "had travelled from Rome to Los Angeles, from there to Washington, and then back across the Atlantic to Belgrade."[35]

In another incident from the Nixon White House, *Newsday* correspondent Martin Schramm found himself the victim of intimidation following the publication of an article critical of the shady dealings of Nixon's close friend Bebe Rebozo. After the story appeared, Schramm was denied access to White House communication director Ron Ziegler. He was also excluded from the press corps that accompanied Nixon on his historic trip to China. Despite its status as a major national paper, *Newsday*'s harassment from the White House lasted for nearly a year until Ziegler proposed to let bygones be bygones on the eve of the 1972 election.[36]

Sometimes intimidation takes the form of challenging the patriotism or the political neutrality of the media, as when Dean Rusk, secretary of state under Lyndon Johnson, challenged the media to defend their coverage of a successful enemy military campaign in Vietnam with this remark: "There gets to be a point when the question is whose side are you on. I'm the Secretary of State, and I'm on our side."[37] Even Thomas Jefferson, the staunchest defender of the press in early America, turned against the papers after he became President.

It is hard to say what the effects of intimidation amount to. At the least, intimidation creates an atmosphere in which every reporter knows that writing an unfavorable story may jeopardize the access to newsmakers on which his or her career depends. At the other extreme, intimidation (or the potential use of it) may grant powerful officials even more news access with which to promote desired political images. One recalls here the words of former NBC president Julian Goodman in response to one of his reporters' complaints about Nixon's excessive use of the TV networks to deliver messages directly to the public. The reporter asked: "Julian, what is your attitude toward President Nixon's requests for television time?" Goodman replied: "Our attitude is the same as our attitude toward previous Presidents: he can have any goddamn thing he wants."[38]

The Effects of News Control

There are several ways to think about the effects of politicians' efforts to control the news. For example, it would be useful to know what proportion of the daily news is directly attributable to official propaganda efforts. It also makes sense to think about the specific political effects of politically loaded versus more detailed, analytical news. Finally, it is worth considering the possible impact of simplistic, repetitive political images on the human capacity to think and reason about politics.

How Much News Is Politically Controlled?

Even a casual look at the daily paper or the nightly news suggests that the bulk of "important" news is devoted to the official actions of the government. The majority of these stories, in turn, seem to be simple condensations of what politicians say and do. In short, the news seems to consist mainly of stories in which at least one point of view is the "official" one. Many stories are framed by two familiar "official" angles—the "Republican" and the "Democrat," for example.

How accurate is this impression that the content of the news is dominated by prepared official messages? Leon Sigal addressed this question in his study of the news content of two of America's finest newspapers, the *New York Times* and the *Washington Post*. If any news outlets would be resistant to the pressures to publish the daily messages of the establishment, it would be these papers. Unlike television and smaller papers, the *Times* and *Post* tend to cover a broad range of national and international affairs in depth. Moreover, they have large reporting staffs, which should free them from dependence on press releases and wire service copy as the scripts for news stories. Finally, the *Times* and *Post* have images as critical liberal papers that are not afraid of exposing government deception. These images are anchored in examples of journalistic independence such as the *Post*'s Watergate coverage and the *Times*' publication of the Pentagon Papers.

How did these bastions of journalism fare against the everyday pressures and temptations to report prepared political information? Not very well. Among Sigal's findings were the following:

- Government officials (either domestic or foreign) were the sources of nearly three quarters of all news, and only one sixth of the news could be traced to sources outside the government. The breakdown of news sources looked like this:[39]

Source	Percent
U.S. officials, agencies	46.5
Foreign, international officials, agencies	27.5
U.S., state, local government officials	4.1
Other news organizations	3.2
Nongovernmental Americans	14.4
Nongovernmental foreigners	2.1
Nonascertainable	2.4

- Less than *1 percent* of all news stories were based on the reporter's own analysis, while over *90 percent* were based on the calculated messages of the actors involved in the situation.[40]

- The vast majority of news stories (from 70 to 90 percent, depending on how they are categorized) are drawn from situations over which newsmakers have either complete or substantial control. Here is the breakdown of the contexts from which the *Times* and *Post* drew their information:[41]

Context	Percent
Press conferences	24.5
Interviews	24.7
Press releases	17.5
Official proceedings	13.0
Background proceedings	7.9
Other nonspontaneous events	4.5
News commentary and editorials	4.0
Leaks	2.3
Nongovernmental proceedings	1.5
Spontaneous events	1.2
Reporter's own analysis	0.9

By any accounting, the conclusion is inescapable: Even the best journalism in the land is extremely dependent on the political messages of a small spectrum of "official" news sources. The *Times* and the *Post*, no doubt, include more detailed background information (not to mention more coverage of obscure events) than most news outlets, but the basic messages in their stories still represent official views. With respect to the substitution of images for information, there is little difference across news outlets. There may be fewer intellectual trappings attached to the images that pulse from the television nightly news, but it is not really clear what the highbrow trappings of the more intellectual print media really accomplish. One suspects that the highbrow media simply make the same images more palatable to people whose self-images require being addressed as sophisticates.

The Political Effects of Controlled News

Perhaps the most obvious political effect of controlled news is the advantage it gives powerful people in getting their issues on the political agenda and defining those issues in ways likely to influence their resolution. Unofficial groups have much more difficulty influencing political outcomes because their perspectives are seldom given credibility via news coverage. As a study of grass-roots organizations by Goldenberg has shown, it is hard for unofficial actors to amass the credibility, resources, and information control necessary to dominate the news long enough to affect the outcomes of issues.[42] When grass-roots groups do make the news, it is often in the contexts of negatively perceived pseudoevents like demonstrations, sit-ins, and other protest activities that may offend the public and draw easy criticism from public officials.

The continuing preference given to narrow official perspectives has an even more serious effect than just influencing the outcomes of specific issues. The long-term effect of politically controlled news is to limit the range of problems, solutions, values, and ideas presented to the American people. The political world becomes a caricature drawn out of unrealistic stereotypes, predictable political postures, and superficial images. The same unworkable solutions are recycled in melodramatic efforts to "solve" chronic problems. People come to accept the existence of problems like poverty, crime, delinquency, war, and political apathy as facts of life rather than as the tragic results of the concentration of political power, the exploitative nature of economic relations, and the cynical uses of political communication. The failure of the news to inform the public about underlying causes of chronic problems creates a sense of helplessness and confusion on the part of those who view politics from the sidelines. The participation of the news media in promoting the official cover stories about these problems further undermines the chances for the kind of public understanding required for effective political action and real political change.

Even when the public officials are caught in acts of blatant deception and misinformation, the result is more likely to create public confusion than to alter the rigid patterns of selecting, defining, and resolving public issues. Short of taking to the streets, people can only watch helplessly when the officials responsible for solving problems are shown to have cynical disregard for the public's need to know the facts and options surrounding those problems. Sometimes the frustrated public is reassured that cases of deception by public officials were justified in order to protect sensitive information for reasons of "national security." Lying, in short, is represented as essential to the public interest. Sometimes people are told that the truth would have been too complex to present to an apathetic and ignorant public. Never mind that apathy and ignorance are probably the results of official deception and neglect. Lying, in short, is represented as the only means of getting the people to grasp the truth. Even when an official becomes genuinely discredited, new images can be created so that his policies can be recycled by successors, as when Lyndon Johnson was driven from the Presidency only to have his unpopular war policies dressed in new images and continued by his successor.

If we add up all the above political effects of images in the news, an even more ominous problem begins to emerge. When people live in a world of images that remove them from reality, there may be enormous pressures to preserve the images at all costs. It is even possible that disproving the facts and assumptions on which images have been built may not always shake the images themselves. In fact, there may be conditions under which discrediting an image may actually strengthen its acceptance. Impossible? Remember the earlier discussion about the weak relationship between image and reality. The thing that makes an image compelling is not sound logic based in objective fact, but its appeal to hopes and fears based in self-fulfilling logic and self-serving fact. There are at least three conditions under which an image may persist in the face of seemingly contradictory evidence.

First, unless a discredited image is replaced with an easy to grasp alternative understanding of a situation, people may find it hard to give up the original image. When people are faced with the choice of replacing a meaningful understanding with nothing, it is hard to sacrifice meaning for meaninglessness. There is ample evidence that people confronted with the loss of meaning may cling even more strongly to their original discredited beliefs. Religious groups that confront the failure of a prophecy often rationalize the failed prophecy as a test of faith and recommit themselves to their beliefs. Similarly, political true believers whose understandings of a problem fail to solve the problem often call for more of the same remedy rather than change their thinking. Thus we have the paradox that solutions may end up worsening the problems they were intended to solve; witness the arms race, the insanity of mental hospitals, the "crime school" atmosphere of prisons, the self-fulfilling nature of welfare, the increasing concentration of wealth following from "trickle down" economic theories, and on and on.

Unfortunately, the news almost never contains new understandings for people to use in replacing dubious images. At best, the news presents the familiar recycled images offered by official opposition groups. Thus, people are faced with an empty choice: Rationalize the continued acceptance of a discredited image or shift to a formerly discredited image that now, by comparison, represents the only meaningful alternative way of understanding the situation. Thus, many disillusioned working-class Democrats voted for Ronald Reagan in 1980 in hopes that his "what's good for big business is good for working people" approach to the economy was viable. Less than a year later, this image was discredited by the factual evidence that many of its principles had failed when put in practice. These millions of people were confronted with the choice of rationalizing the failures of "Reaganomics" or returning to the familiar Democratic image of the "welfare state" economy that had been discredited in their minds only a year before. Psychologists tell us that the persistent adoption of nonfunctional understandings in our everyday lives produces at best neurosis and at worst can lead to schizophrenia, paranoia, and other psychoses. Perhaps it is a good thing that people are not encouraged to incorporate politics as a central part of their lives.

A second factor that might lead to the continued effectiveness of a seemingly discredited image is that the discrediting often places people in the difficult position of not knowing which authority to believe. Should they accept the public official who denies having misled the public, or should they accept the news media's impartial reporting of the allegations of some other equally authoritative official? Since neither version of the truth brings the public any closer to the actual situation, the truth becomes hard to determine, not to mention irrelevant. For example, in the early stages of U.S. political and military involvement in El Salvador, the government publicized a State Department "white paper" titled "Communist Interference in El Salvador." The report laid the foundation for an image of Soviet-provoked revolution in El Salvador. The report contained many factual errors and unsupported claims, none of which prevented the State Department from releasing it as headline-making news. The *Wall Street Journal* (hardly a liberal mouthpiece) published an article pointing out the flaws in the report and noting an admission by the report's author that parts of the white paper were "misleading."[43] Following the article's publication, the State Department issued an attack on the *Wall Street Journal* denying that the author of the white paper had discredited his own report and calling the report "an accurate and honest description of Communist support for the Salvadoran insurgency."[44] At that point, the news story was closed. The *Journal* defended itself in an editorial, and the public was left with the choice of who to believe: the U.S. Department of State or one newspaper's reporter.

The next phase of the government's efforts to build a case for its involvement in El Salvador took advantage of the same means of maintaining support for an image contradicted by observable reality. U.S. military aid to El Salvador was tied by law to the Salvadoran government's observance of certain human rights standards. Therefore, it was not in the interest of the Reagan administration to admit that the Salvadorans had committed numerous atrocities that made a mockery of the human rights concern. For the nearly six months between the release of the white paper and crucial congressional hearings on the question of military aid to El Salvador, there were numerous reports in the news of atrocities committed by the Salvadoran government against thousands of its own citizens: torture, mass murder, destruction of villages, rape, and other acts of terrorism. At that time, however, American reporters were not present in the war zone, and neither government would admit that such atrocities had occurred. Thus the reports were labeled in the news as "unconfirmed reports" even by such liberal news outlets as National Public Radio.[45]

Why? Because the U.S. government refused to "confirm" those reports (even though the subsequent congressional testimony indicated that the State Department had documentation of thousands of human rights violations), and the Salvadoran government defined the incidents in such symbolic terms as "successful search and destroy missions against known terrorists."[46] Thus the favorable image of a corrupt political regime was kept alive by pitting the official positions of the governments against "unconfirmed reports" from unknown sources. The irony, of course, is that the news media depended on the government to discredit its own image. Under those paradoxical conditions, what was the public to believe— uncertain facts, or such familiar official statements as the State Department's dramatic claim that "the decisive battle for Central America is now under way in El Salvador. If, after Nicaragua, the government of El Salvador is captured by a violent minority, who in Latin America will live without fear?"[47]

A third condition that can lead to the continued effectiveness of an image even in the face of apparent evidence to the contrary is when the initial message on which the image was built remains more salient than subsequent disclosures of contradictory evidence. Since the media depend on cues from news sources to determine the bigness of stories, an initial story may receive intensive coverage simply because it was a well-constructed pseudoevent. Follow-up stories pointing out errors may be based on reporters' own initiatives, and as such have less clear-cut claims to prominent coverage. Moreover, since facts generally take the back seat in the news to more abstract images, it is not always clear how factual contradictions ought to fit into a story. The most obvious exception, of course, is when the contradiction is pointed out by a political opponent, thereby providing a script for a standard news formula.

An example showing how documented factual errors can fail to receive as much coverage as the original story occurred in the aftermath of a Reagan press conference in which several key messages from the President were bolstered by erroneous evidence. Reporters had become annoyed at Reagan's use of dubious information to support his political messages. Several reporters set out to investigate the claims made at the press conference. It was later found that a statement about tithing 10 percent of his income to charities and worthy causes was untrue—he had contributed none of his income to charities. Also shown to be untrue was his claim that state-funded abortions in California had increased dramatically when women were allowed to use rape as an "excuse" for abortion. In fact, a sweeping reform in California assistance programs, not the admission of the "rape excuse," accounted for the California abortion increase. Reagan also cited the case of an Arizona welfare program that had increased its services and lowered its costs by turning to private sector support—claims that were denied by the director of the program.[48] By any measure, these corrections were given less prominent coverage than Reagan's original messages in which the statements in question appeared. More important, the facts were challenged through personalized news stories about Reagan rather than in stories aimed at the political images that the facts might have helped to inspire.

There was a postscript to the above story. As suggested earlier, politicians monitor the news closely in the daily battle to protect their images. Minor though the media criticisms might have been, they were not lost on Reagan. At his next press conference, a reporter began to question the source for one of Reagan's patented claims of factual proof. Anticipating such an incident, Reagan drew a folded sheet of paper from his coat pocket and said it contained proof of his earlier statements. He then admonished the press for questioning the statements challenged following his last press conference. When asked by reporters to reveal that proof, he refused to do so. Reagan clearly understood that in the news, facts are incidental to images—even images about facts. Rather than introduce facts that might not have ended the matter (even if they existed), he simply invoked a condition favorable to maintaining an image about his facts. By holding up the mysterious sheet of paper, he in effect asked the audience, "Who do you want to believe here, your President or these reporters?" Thus, the conditions that bolster faltering images can operate together to prop up even the most dubious of images.

The Impact on the Public

What are the human consequences of a political world in which contradictions are commonplace, facts are incidental, and meanings are cranked out by formula? Because of the shocking absence of research on this question, we can only speculate. Our speculation need not be of the idle sort, however. There is a lot of "homeless" data about the political profiles of the American public. I say "homeless" because we have amassed a great many facts about the politics of the average citizen without really offering very convincing explanations for those facts. Why, for example, are most people so apathetic politically? Why do people seem to change their political views so readily and then cling to them so strongly, only to change them again just as suddenly? Why do people seem unable to think clearly and critically about politics?

These and other related questions lie at the center of a puzzle surrounding American politics. If America is truly the world's strongest democracy, why do the people take so little initiative in formulating problems and solving them? The easy answer is that people are by nature apathetic, fickle, and ignorant. Even if such untestable assertions were true, they would not contain adequate answers to the puzzle of American democracy. Why, for example, are people who are so fanatical about sports, entertainment, or religion so apathetic about politics? How can people with such well-developed views of religion or society be so confused about politics?

If, in fact, our main experience of the political world is created by political actors as food for our imaginations, and if these experiences are filtered through the medium of news before they reach us, then we may have the clues necessary to solve these mysteries. As mentioned earlier, people tend to become helpless when they encounter inconsistent, changing, and unworkable explanations for life's problems. In fact, helplessness becomes a learned survival skill in capricious environments. Have we, perhaps, confused the signs of learned political helplessness by calling it "apathy"? Similarly, when people are constantly presented with the choice between a familiar explanation of a situation and no explanation, they usually opt for familiarity, no matter how empty or irrelevant it may be. Meaning, even when it becomes perverse, is a hard thing to do without. Thus, when each failed approach to chronic problems is supplanted by equally failed but familiar past approaches, should people be expected to choose nothingness instead? This raises the question whether people change their political minds readily, or do they, in effect, have their minds changed for them? Finally, when people are confronted with ideas that contain little in the way of intellectual challenge, thought-provoking logic, or credible opposition (save other official sources promoting their own empty images), it is hardly surprising that the average person is not very articulate about politics. Ask a fan why her team lost the championship or ask a farmer about the effects of commodities markets on crop prices, and you will hear thoughtful replies. Ask a citizen about the economy, and you will probably hear the sixty seconds of pro or con rationalizations that have become the formulas for news stories on the subject. Sometimes, of course, you will not even hear this simplistic formula because when images really succeed, words, like facts, become incidental.

Solutions?

This book concludes with a formal proposal for solving some of the problems with the news that have been discussed thus far. At this point, however, at least one solution seems pretty obvious. Since we have a free press, why cannot the media just stop reporting news based on events produced clearly for propaganda purposes? After all, it seems that nearly every time journalists get together to talk about the news, they vow to stop being victimized by public officials with their staged events. Every election, for example, is a time of renewal for the news media. *TV Guide* magazine was just one of the media outlets that jumped on the perennial bandwagon of news reform in 1976 when it issued a press release publicizing a forthcoming special story on news reform. Despite its tone of immediacy, the *Guide*'s press release had the quality of a timeless news script, beginning with the opening statement:

> RADNOR, PA–News officials of the three major TV networks say they will concentrate their 1976 Presidential election coverage more on issues than on personalities, *TV Guide* magazine reported today.
>
> News executives admitted that they have learned from past mistakes and all are agreed this year against putting too much emphasis on the candidates themselves and too little on the issues.
>
> "We are not going to be taken in by all the media events. We are trying to get substance," said Richard Salant, President of CBS News.[49]

What happened in 1976? Jimmy Carter was elected President on the strength of one of the most image-laden, pseudoevent-based campaigns in American history. How were the images transmitted to the voters? Largely through the news, of course. The media seized upon Carter as a new face who obliged them with a deluge of personality-oriented pseudo-events that were ideal for the personalized coverage of a very dramatic (even if irrelevant) headline news plot: *Virtual Unknown Comes Out of Nowhere To Nab Presidency*.

So much for the perennial good intentions of journalism to reform itself. In between the periodic outbreaks of self-criticism, the news business runs along its familiar course of reporting the news that newsmakers make. Journalists who might criticize their product during reflective moments seem to accept it as routine and legitimate when confronted with a deadline to meet. When the light of self-criticism is off, some in the news business can even be heard to chide newsmakers who fail to manipulate the press cleverly enough. Pseudonews has become so entrenched that reporters seem to have a certain respect for officials who manipulate the news effectively while holding in contempt those officials who fail to control the news. A case in point was reporter David Broder's postmortem on candidate John Anderson's poor showing in the 1980 election. The cause of Anderson's political death? In Broder's words, "he did little to shape the coverage of his campaign."[50] This gap between journalistic ideals and reporting realities is too large to go unexplained. The reasons why journalists cooperate in the reporting of politicized news is the subject of the next chapter.

Notes

1. Cited from William Pfaff, "Yalta Only Symbol," *Seattle Post Intelligencer*, 26 January 1982, p. All.
2. Dean Acheson, *Present at the Creation: My Years in the State Department* (New York: Norton, 1969), p. 375.
3. See W. Lance Bennett, Patricia Dempsey Harris, Janet K. Laskey, Alan H. Levitch, and Sarah E. Monrad, "Deep and Surface Images in the Construction of Political Issues: The Case of Amnesty," *Quarterly Journal of Speech*, 62 (April 1976): 109–26.
4. See Bruce Miroff, *Pragmatic Illusions: The Presidential Politics of John F. Kennedy* (New York: Longman, 1976).
5. See David Wise, *The Politics of Lying* (New York: Vintage, 1973).
6. See William Greider, "The Education of David Stockman," *Atlantic Monthly*, December 1981, pp. 27–54.
7. See Richard Barnet, *Roots of War* (Baltimore: Penguin, 1972).
8. For a more detailed discussion of this incident, see Wise, *The Politics of Lying*, chap. 5.
9. Walter Lippmann, *Public Opinion* (New York: Free Press, 1922), p. 9.
10. Acheson, *Present at the Creation*, p. 375.
11. See Murray Edelman, *Political Language* (New York: Academic Press, 1977).
12. Quoted by F. Christopher Arterton, "Campaign Organizations Face the Mass Media in the 1976 Presidential Nomination Process" (paper presented at the meeting of the American Political Science Association, Washington, D.C., September 1977), p. 4.
13. NBC News "White Paper" on the Reagan Presidency; 30 December 1981.
14. For a detailed discussion of how this worked, see Joe McGinniss, *The Selling of the President* (New York: Pocket Books, 1969).
15. David L. Paletz and Robert M. Entman, *Media Power Politics* (New York: Free Press, 1981), pp. 69–70.
16. Ibid., p. 70.
17. Ibid., p. 66.
18. Ibid., pp. 66–68.
19. Wise, *The Politics of Lying*.
20. David R. Mayhew, *Congress: The Electoral Connection* (New Haven: Yale University Press, 1974).
21. See William J. Fulbright, *The Pentagon Propaganda Machine* (New York: Vintage, 1970); also Barnet, *Roots of War*.
22. Wise, *Politics of Lying*.
23. Ibid., p. 273.
24. For the classic discussion of symbols in politics, see Murray Edelman, *The Symbolic Uses of Politics* (Champagne-Urbana: University of Illinois Press, 1964).
25. This incident involved the Bellevue, Washington, police department and was reported on KIRO News Radio, Seattle, Wash., 16 February 1982.
26. UPI wire story, reported in the *Seattle Post-Intelligencer*, 26 September 1979, p. A2.

27. Reported over KNX News Radio, Los Angeles, Calif., date lost.
28. AP wire story reported in the *Seattle Post-Intelligencer*, 19 October 1981, p. 1.
29. Daniel Boorstin, *The Image: A Guide to Pseudo-Events in America* (New York: Atheneum, 1961).
30. Harvey Molotch and Marilyn Lester, "Accidents, Scandals, and Routines: Resources for Insurgent Methodology," in *The TV Establishment*, ed. Gaye Tuchman (Englewood Cliffs, N.J.: Prentice-Hall, 1974), p. 55.
31. Boorstin, *The Image*, pp. 11–12.
32. David Wise, *Politics of Lying*, pp. 3–16.
33. Reported in Paletz and Entman, *Media Power Politics*, p. 40.
34. Associated Press wire story, *Seattle Times*, 8 February 1982, p. A3.
35. From Wise, *Politics of Lying*, p. 348.
36. Ibid., pp. 317–25.
37. Ibid., p. 455.
38. Ibid., p. 368.
39. Leon V. Sigal, *Reporters and Officials: The Organization and Politics of News Reporting* (Lexington, Mass.: Heath, 1973), p.124.
40. Ibid., p. 122.
41. Ibid.
42. Edie Goldenberg, *Making the Papers* (Lexington, Mass.: Heath-Lexington Books, 1975).
43. Jonathan Kwitney, "Apparent Errors Cloud U.S. 'White Paper' on Reds in El Salvador," *Wall Street Journal*, 8 June 1981, p. 1.
44. Frederick Taylor, "The El Salvador 'White Paper,'" *Wall Street Journal*, 21 August 1981, p. 22.
45. NPR "Morning Edition," 1 February 1982.
46. Reported on "NBC Nightly News," 1 February 1982.
47. Statement by U.S. Undersecretary of State Thomas Enders on "NBC Nightly News," 1 February 1982.
48. These and other errors were reported by CBS anchor Diane Sawyer on the "CBS Morning News," 19 January 1982.
49. *TV Guide*–prepared *News Release* (Radnor, Pa.: Triangle Publications, 20 April 1976).
50. David S. Broder, "All Platform, No Campaign?" *Washington Post*, 7 September 1980, p. D4.

THREE

Journalists and Political Reporting

> ... people may expect too much of journalism. Not only do they expect it to be entertaining, they expect it to be true.
>
> LEWIS LAPHAM

It is obvious why politicians attempt to control the news. It is less clear why journalists report so much politically loaded information. If the American news media were state controlled or noncompetitive, it would be easy to excuse reporters for passing along, without comment, the political messages in news events. The emphasis given to official views in the news is less excusable when the American news media are proclaimed to be free agents operating in a political system that values free speech. How can we reconcile the official bias of the news with the common assumptions that the media are (or at least have the potential to be) objective, independent, professional, and even adversarial in their relations with news sources?

The problem of a "free press" dutifully reporting what officials dictate is so perplexing that a number of theories in communication, sociology, and political science have addressed the situation. Although each explanation proposes a different specific reason, they all seem to agree that the general answer has something to do with the routine newsgathering practices of reporters and their news organizations. It is increasingly clear that the everyday work routines of the media bias the news in favor of official views without really intending to do so. Our first order of business, then, is to show how the everyday practices of journalists and their news organizations contribute to "normalized" (not to mention "personalized," "dramatized," and "fragmented") news.

In addition to explaining how reporting practices bias the news, it is important to understand why these habits persist and why neither the press nor the public seems to grasp their true political effects. For example, many members of the press continue to defend their reporting habits as being largely consistent with the professional journalism norms of independence and objectivity. In the light of this common defense of standard journalistic practices, it is worth taking a look at the real meaning of professional norms like independence and objectivity. At times, of course, these professional ideals have served both the press and the public well. In a few celebrated cases, reporters and editors have even gone to jail in order to protect the confidentiality of sources or defend the principle that government secrets should not be kept from the American people. In many respects, however, the professional norms of independence and objectivity have backfired. In fact, it can be shown that journalists have become trapped within an unworkable set of professional standards, with the result that the more "objective" reporters try to be, the more official bias they introduce into the news. The second order of business is to show how the professional code of the press perpetuates the problems it is supposed to prevent.

How Reporting Practices Contribute to News Bias

Much like any job, reporting the news consists largely of a set of routine, standardized activities. Despite some obvious differences involving the nature of assignments and personal writing styles, reporters tend to cover news events in remarkably similar ways. The existence of standardized reporting behaviors and story formulas is not surprising when one considers the strong patterns of constraints that operate in the news environment. For example, the events staged by political actors tend to reflect the predictable political communication goals outlined in the last chapter. Moreover, most mass media news organizations tend to impose fairly similar constraints on reporters in terms of acceptable story angles, deadlines, and newsgathering resources. It is also the case that reporters are subjected to the standardizing influence of working in close quarters with one another, covering the same sorts of events under the same kinds of pressures. In short, reporters confront three separate sources of pressure to standardize their reporting habits: pressures from news sources, pressures from news organizations, and pressures from fellow reporters. Each of these forces in the news environment contributes to the development of standardized reporting formulas that favor the incorporation of official political messages in the news and that lead reporters to write personalized, dramatized, and fragmented news stories.

Reporters and Officials: Pressures to Cooperate

Most political events are so predictably scripted that reporters can condense them easily into formula plot outlines: *who* (which official) did *what*
(official action), *where* (in what official setting), for what (officially
stated) *purpose*, and with what (officially proclaimed) *result*. For example:

> President _____ met at the White House today with President _____ of
> _____ to discuss mutual concerns about _____. Both leaders called the
> talks productive and said that important matters were resolved.

It does not take a careful reading to see that such a formula is virtually
devoid of substance. The pseudoevents that provide the scripts for such
news stories are generally designed to create emotionally appealing images, not to transmit substantive information about real political issues.
Since such events are routine political occurrences, reporters quickly develop formulas for converting them into news whenever they occur. Com-
pounding the temptation to report official versions of political events is
the fact that reporters live in a world where "divide and conquer" is an
ever-present part of life. Careers are advanced by receiving scoops and
leaks; careers are damaged by being left out in the cold and excluded
from official contact. Like it or not, reporters are dependent on the
sources they cover. When those sources are powerful officials surrounded
by an entourage of eager reporters clamoring for news, there is the constant possibility that those who report what officials want them to will be
rewarded, while those who fail to convert key political messages into
news will be punished.

In view of the patterned nature of political events, combined with the
possibility of divide and conquer tactics from politicians, it is not surprising that the news seems to emerge from formulas that virtually write
themselves.[1] Of course, knowing the formulas does not mean that reporters will always use them. However, in a workday world filled with short
deadlines, demanding editors, and persuasive news sources, the formulas
become the course of least resistance. Even when a formula is abandoned, there is seldom enough other information floating around in a
typical political setting to construct another story. In the illusory world of
political news, formulas describe "official" actions, and the seal of "official" approval becomes a substitute for truth and authenticity, which in
turn makes the formulas seem legitimate.[2]

In addition to developing work habits that favor official views, reporters are also human beings. Behind the occupational roles are people who
sometimes identify with the newsmakers they cover. Regular contact
under stressful conditions makes it easy to see officials as sympathetic

characters faced with seemingly insurmountable obstacles in their efforts to do the right thing—not the least of those obstacles being a hostile pack of reporters. Of course, when officials go out of their way to antagonize the press, as the Nixon administration did during the early 1970s, it is more difficult for reporters to experience feelings of sympathy and identification. When officials court the favor and understanding of reporters, they are often paid back with favorable coverage that sticks close to the official's political line.[3] Such coverage is easily justified as an "objective" account of the official's public actions.

Reporters who are not possessed by such human sympathy may succumb to another, less altruistic, personal motive to report the official line. Journalists who cooperate with powerful officials are often recognized, flattered, and taken into the confidence of those officials. In the intensely political environments that generate most of our news, nothing is valued as much as power. If one cannot possess power (and there always seems to be a shortage), then the next best thing is to be on the "inside" with the powerful—to be seen with them, to be consulted by them, to socialize with them, perhaps even to have them as friends. As Tom Bethell put it, to be on close terms with elite news sources "is to be an 'insider,' which is what almost everyone in Washington wants to be. It is interesting to note how often this word appears on the dust jackets of memoirs by Washington journalists. But Nixon—his great weakness!—didn't like journalists and wouldn't let them be insiders. ... Kissinger, on the other hand, was astute enough to cultivate the press, and he survived—not merely that, was lionized as 'the wizard of shuttle diplomacy.' (Is it not possible that the most awesome 'lesson of Watergate' ... will be a social lesson?)"[4] As the distinguished reporter Murray Kempton put it: "It is a fundamental fact about journalism, and might even be a rule if it had the attention it deserves, that it is next to impossible to judge any public figure with the proper detachment once you begin calling him by his first name."[5]

Reporters as Members of News Organizations: Pressures to Standardize

If their relations with officials set news formulas in motion, reporters' own news organizations reinforce the use of those formulas. Novice journalists experience constant pressures (subtle and otherwise) from editors about how to cover stories.[6] These pressures are effective because editors hold sway over what becomes news and which reporters advance in the organization. Over time, reporters tend to adjust their styles to fit harmoniously with the expectations of their organizations.

Why do editors, publishers, and TV news producers favor the "documentary" reporting of official events? In part, because standardized news is safe. People in managerial posts in news organizations must constantly compare their product with the competition and defend "risky" departures from the reporting norm. As Epstein observed in his study of television network news, even TV news assignment editors look to the conservative wire services for leads on stories and angles for reporting them.[7] The wires establish a baseline for the day's news. Despite (or, as is more likely, because of) the fact that the wires cover the highest portion of planned official events and stick closest to official political scripts, they set the tone for each day's news. Following the daily lead of the wires becomes the most efficient and easiest to defend method of charting the day's reporting assignments.

Although the conservatism of editors (Lou Grant and Ben Bradlee forgive me) is the most immediate factor reinforcing reporters' use of news formulas, other organizational arrangements may have an even stronger influence on standardized reporting. Among the most powerful standardizing forces are daily news production routines. Newspapers and news programs require a minimum supply of news every day whether or not anything significant happens in the world. Perhaps you have seen a television news program on a "slow news day." In place of the usual stream of international crises, press conferences, congressional hearings, and proclamations by the mayor, the news may consist of a trip to the zoo to visit a new "baby," a canned report on acupuncture in China, a follow-up story on the survivor of an air crash, and a film spoof on the opening of baseball spring training in Florida. Slow news days occur during weekends, holidays, vacation periods, or recesses when governments are closed down. News organizations are ill equipped to handle slow days because their daily routines are geared to reporting the official happenings from the news centers of the world.

In order for a news organization to function, it must fill up a minimum "news hole" every day. It must do this on schedule and in an efficient way. Producing a large amount of cheap, predictable news normally means assigning reporters to events and beats that are sure to produce enough acceptable stories to fill up the news hole by the day's deadline. During normal business periods, the public relations machinery of government and business are only too happy to comply with these organizational needs by producing events that are cheap, easy to report, numerous, and predictable. Reporters, in short, are given assignments based largely on the routine news requirements of their organizations. The resulting patterns of contact between reporters and news sources reinforce the use of standard reporting formulas.

Filling up the daily "news hole" on time means that news organizations must figure out how to make the spontaneous more predictable. The obvious solution to this problem is to anticipate when and where the required amount of news will happen every day. Since this task is made difficult by the size of the world and the smallness of reporting staffs, the solution is to adjust the definition of news (implicitly of course) so that things that are known to happen on a regular basis become news. Hence, reporters can be assigned to cover those things and be assured (by definition) of gathering news every day. As a result, the backbone of the news organization is the network of "beats," ranging from the police station and the city council at the local level to Congress, Court, and Presidency at the national level. These beats produce each day's familiar run of murders, robberies, fires, accidents, public hearings, press conferences, and shots of the President entering helicopters and leaving airplanes.

To break the daily routine, some reporters are given special assignments to cover big stories like the Iranian hostage crisis or spontaneous events like assassinations and floods. However, the expense of special-assignment coverage dictates that even the truly spontaneous must be translated into familiar formulas. If an event is important enough to justify special coverage, then it must be represented in dramatic terms. Even assassinations and floods quickly become scripted. For example, an assassination story will always include such basic dramatic ingredients as elaborate scenic descriptions, information about who did it, a report on the condition of the leader, a description of what happened to the assassin, and speculation about who's in charge politically. A flood story also demands dramatic pictures and detailed scenic descriptions accompanied by accounts of the damage and human suffering, followed by a description of relief efforts, and concluding with an assessment of whether things will get better or worse.

In addition to beats and special-coverage assignments, many large news organizations have developed a third newsgathering unit, the geographically assigned crew. For example, television networks have news crews (correspondent, video and sound technicians) stationed in large cities like Chicago, New York, Houston, Los Angeles, and Miami. The assumption is that enough "news" will be generated from these areas to warrant assigning personnel to them. The use of geographical assignments reflects another way in which organizational routines have shaped the definition of news into a convenient formula. Since national news cannot all come from Washington, reporters must be assigned to other locations. But what other locations? Any location chosen suddenly becomes a defining center for "national news." As Epstein discovered in his study of television network news, almost all non-Washington news originates from the handful of cities where the networks station their crews.[8] One explanation for the choice of cities like Chicago and Houston for crew assignments is that these are major cities where important things happen. Another explanation for the way the networks (and to a lesser extent, the wire services) round out their national newsgathering is that communication and news production facilities are cheaper and more accessible in major centers of commerce than in more out-of-the-way cities. For example, it is more efficient to feed stories from Los Angeles to New York than from Seattle to New York. As a result, the news becomes still more standardized, with events in a few centers of politics and commerce given much more play than events elsewhere, regardless of their newsworthiness. Of course, if Seattle falls into the ocean, it will be covered as readily as when Los Angeles falls into the ocean, but a speech by the vice president or even the President in Seattle is less likely to be covered than the same speech delivered in Los Angeles, Chicago, New York, Houston, or Miami. Ever wonder why so many speeches are given in Los Angeles, Chicago, New York, Houston, and Miami?

The Paradox of Organizational Routines

The only problem with routine newsgathering is that all the news starts looking pretty much the same. This would not be so bad if one news organization monopolized all the news, since the audience would not have choices to worry about. However, there are many papers, radio programs, and television broadcasts from which to receive the daily news. It is hard to establish a competitive edge in the news market when the efforts of news organizations to make news production more efficient also make the news pretty much the same no matter which major paper one reads or which channel is tuned in. In short, routine news may be efficient, but it limits the share of the market that any media source can capture. For example, if all the news on television is pretty much the same, all other things being equal, each network should capture an equal share of the audience. Thus, efficiency may end up imposing an unintended ceiling on audience share, which limits the growth of profits in the news organization—and news is, after all, a big business.

The news industry has created a serious dilemma for itself. Changing news formulas in order to produce more distinctive, competitive news would end up costing more, which would reduce efficiency, which would reduce profits. Increasing the audience share is pointless if profits decrease in the process. This problem has led many other industries to "stabilize," with each competing producer settling for a fixed market share because the methods required to expand the market would actually decrease profits. Examples of market stabilization abound in such industries as automobiles, steel, agriculture, and food products, just to name a few. Another reason why breaking out of the news routine has not been attractive to news organizations is that it is not clear what the alternative would look like even if it were profitable to worry about it. Since news is largely the product of convenient conventions between politicians and journalists, it is not clear where to look for guidance in reforming the product. Any new format would surely draw criticism from politicians and other news organizations, and it might startle the public, risking the possible loss of audience share. As a result, tampering too much with the standard newsgathering routines is not something that the media like to think about. However, the media also find it hard to settle for fixed shares of such a lucrative market.

The economic dilemma of how to sell routine news has been resolved by the emergence of a growing industry of media consultant firms that advise radio and television stations and, increasingly, newspapers, on how to expand the news audience and increase profits at the same time. "News doctors" like Yankelovich, Skelly and White, and Frank Magid sell expensive audience analyses to news organizations much like marketing firms sell market analyses to the producers of toothpastes, deodorants, and hemorrhoid preparations.

Unfortunately for the news consumer, the entry of news doctors into the news business only increases the emphasis on formula news. As pointed out in Chapter 1, most marketing advice involves the promotion of style over substance. Hence it is more likely that the major network news programs will refrain from altering their news content if there are changes that can be made in reporters, anchor personalities, theme music, or sets. Even when changes are made in news content, they are unlikely to alter the basic political messages that are locked into the news formula. For example, "CBS Evening News" introduced a special-feature report in its newscast. The only notable difference between those special reports and regular news stories was that the special segments were somewhat longer than typical news stories—a stylistic rather than substantive change.

Instead of eliminating the formulas on which market efficiency and smooth news production depend, the news doctors specialize in "format cosmetics," such as dressing up formula reporting with different delivery styles, introducing new gimmicks into old formulas (e.g., "live helicopter coverage"), and determining what mix of formulas will work best in a particular market.[9] For example, Channel 5 in Metropolis, Illinois, might be encouraged to downplay dull coverage of city council hearings and run more crime stories because the news doctor's survey shows that people in town are particularly concerned about crime these days (and will surely be even more concerned after the number of crime stories increases). Meanwhile, Channel 4 in Pleasantville, New Mexico, is told that people are tired of crime stories but might be receptive to more news featuring local characters, scenes, and events. (The news doctor's survey shows that the people of Pleasantville have an unusual degree of civic pride, and a news program that tapped those attitudes would attract a larger and more loyal audience.) In East Egg, New York, the advice may be to buy a helicopter and expensive remote-transmission equipment so that Channel 3 can do more live stories. Even though very few meaningful things happen "live" at 6:00 p.m., the use of live action at the top of the news will distinguish Channel 3 in style, if not in substance, from its competition. Meanwhile, Channel 8 in Sprocket, Nebraska, is advised to add a 6:30 a.m. local newscast to its already lengthy news schedule. A survey has shown that people are "hungry" for news at that hour and no other TV station has tapped the market. In Capitol City, Georgia, Channel 2 is advised to rerun the 11:00 p.m. news at 2:00 in the morning because large numbers of swing-shift workers at local factories constitute an as yet untapped market for the news. The advice to Channel 11 in Nirvanna, California, is to fire the aging and stodgy anchorman and hire an attractive but not too sexy younger female anchorperson.

And so it goes, a new face here, a new set there, here a format, there a helicopter, more crime, less city hall, more local color, more pictures, fewer talking heads, shorter stories, more weather (weather is becoming very big). And how about a hard-hitting political commentator to go with that new "action" image? When a news doctor enters the scene, the patient can receive anything from minor surgery to a complete program transplant, depending on how much the news organization can afford and how serious the problem is. A typical media consultant's services will include a survey of the tastes and habits of the news audience, some specific audience responses to the client's program or paper (usually through standard marketing techniques involving small "focus group" discussions), an assessment of the competition, an analysis of the current news organization, and a set of recommendations to company management about how to "enhance" the news product.

Such services are expensive, and the resulting advice is not easily dismissed. News organizations across the country are increasingly faced with the choice of buying a news prescription designed to keep them in sound financial health or falling behind in the news image game to organizations that are more willing to buy helicopters, remote equipment, high-salaried reporters, attractive anchor people, and the news formulas geared to the tastes of the audience.

Even the newspaper, long the elite bastion of journalism standards, has succumbed to the formulas of the news doctors. One study found that between 1950 and 1970 the average American newspaper grew in length from 34 pages to 54 pages, while average hard news content dropped from 11.1 to 8.8 percent.[10] When the revered *New York Times* changed its format in 1976, a before-and-after comparison indicated that local and national coverage were down by 11 percent and 30 percent, respectively, while society and women's sections surged by 80 percent.[11] One newspaper revamped its entire format and called itself "The Newspaper for People Who Watch Television." In a typical edition of that tabloid, national and international news were boiled down to a column of "briefs" on page 2, while the front page featured a human interest story about a recluse living without modern conveniences.[12]

It seems that the news doctors have produced two unfortunate results: the more effective deployment of standard political formulas and the general deemphasis of politics in favor of human interest irrelevancies. There seems to be little resistance to these trends from the decision makers of news organizations. After receiving a survey of audience reading habits, the management of one major daily paper is reported to have issued a memo to reporters calling for more "fine examples" of rapes, robberies, and auto accidents on page 1.[13] Whether the news doctor's cure involves more human interest stories or more stereotyped coverage of political heroes in action, the result is the same as far as political information goes: The news hinders rather than helps people understand the important events in their world.

The contribution of the news doctors to standardized news obviously raises a number of important questions, including the following:

1. Is the news anything more than the collection of arbitrary (at best) or most profitable (at worst) formula stories selected by news organizations to fill their daily quotas?
2. Should news be based on market considerations, or should it be based on some independent criteria of importance and newsworthiness?
3. Just because people admit to watching or reading news about fires, murders, accidents, and political heroes, does this necessarily mean that
   a. They want more of it?
   b. They think these things are important?
   c. They think these things belong in the news?
   d. They would not prefer alternative, nonformula news more?
   e. They might be more engaged by news that actually explains human events instead of news that promotes political messages and recounts real life melodrama?

Such questions are dodged by news doctors and media executives, who reply simplistically that they are interested only in making the news more relevant to people. It is doubtful that current marketing surveys really measure popular demand at all.[14] For example, most media surveys are designed with the assumption that formula news is a given. Audiences are not asked if they would prefer alternatives to formula news, they are simply asked which news formulas they like best. Market research that might turn up results damaging to product efficiency would defeat the purpose of the news doctors. Thus the standard excuse that the news reflects what the people want might be stated more properly as *"the news reflects what people prefer among those choices that we find profitable and convenient to offer them."* This is not the same thing as saying that the news is responsive to popular demand. Thus, whether we look at standard organizational routines or the efforts of news organizations to "upgrade" their product, we find factors that reinforce the familiar trends toward more normalized news, more fragmented news, more dramatic news, and more personalized news.

Reporters as a Pack: Pressures to Agree

As a result of the increasingly routine nature of newsgathering, reporters tend to move in packs. They are assigned together to the same events and the same beats. More than most workers, they share close social experiences on the job. Together they eat, sleep, travel, drink, and wait, and wait, and wait. As a result of such intimate social contact, reporters tend to develop a sense of solidarity. They learn to cope with shared pressures from news organizations and news sources. They come to accept news formulas as inevitable, even though they may express cynical complaints about them in between mad scrambles to meet deadlines. They respect one another as independent professionals, but engage in the social courtesies of comparing notes and corroborating story angles.

This profile of the reporter's social world was called "pack journalism" by Timothy Crouse in his insightful description of press coverage during the 1972 election.[15] He concluded that reporters come into such close contact, under such sympathetic conditions, while covering such controlled events, that they do not have to collaborate formally in order to end up reporting things the same way. Once a reporter has been assigned to a routine event for which news formulas are well known, the temptation to produce a formula story is bound to be strong. Add to this temptation the presence of a tight deadline and an editor who will question significant departures from the formula used by other reporters, and the temptation to standardize becomes even stronger. Finally, put the reporter in a group of sympathetic human beings faced with the same temptations, and the use of formulas becomes easily rationalized and accepted with the social support of the group.

So strong are the pressures of the pack that they have been felt even by a trained sociologist who posed as a reporter in order to study newsgathering from an insider's perspective. While working as a reporter for a small daily paper, Mark Fishman was assigned to the city council beat. He quickly fit into the routine of writing formula stories that mirrored the council's careful efforts to create an image of democracy in action— complete with elaborate hearings, citizen input, serious deliberations, and formal votes. In a rare case when an issue before the council got out of control and turned into a hot political argument, the reporters at the press table reacted strangely. Instead of seizing the issue as the hottest news of the day, they ignored it. Ignoring a bit of news that did not fit the mold took some social prompting from various members of the "pack." As Fishman described it, "the four members of the press (including Fishman) were showing increasing signs of impatience with the controversy. At first the reporters stopped taking notes; then they began showing their dis- approval to each other; finally, they were making jokes about the foolish- ness of the debate. No evidence could be found in their comments that they considered the controversy anything other than a stupid debate over a trivial matter unworthy of the time and energy the council put into it."[16] Fishman noted the strength of group pressure operating against indepen- dent news judgment: "Even though at the time of the incident I was sitting at the press table (as a reporter) making derisive comments about the foolishness of the council along with other journalists, it occurred to me later how this controversy could be seen as an important event in city hall."[17]

Just as Fishman succumbed to the pressures of the "pack" and still recognized them at a conscious level, most reporters are aware of group pressure but seem unable to escape it. In a study of the Washington jour- nalism corps, the nation's reporting elite, Hess found that pack journal- ism was regarded by reporters as the most serious problem they faced.[18] As Hess noted, however, the social conditions of pack journalism will persist as long as news organizations establish their routines around the predictable actions of officials. Perhaps more important, such reporting routines are likely to persist as long as they can be rationalized in terms of the professional standard of "objective" reporting.

Professional Journalism Standards and News Bias: Why Objective Reporting Is Not Objective

The reporting routines described in the last section are not often regarded by journalists or the public as sources of political bias in the news. To the contrary, they are often taken as signs of an independent, professional press in America. The existence of beats, special-assignment coverage, and regional news crews can be defended as the broadest possible "news net"—a net that assures coverage of virtually everything that happens. Story formulas can be represented as comprehensive documentary accounts of observable events. Competition among news organizations for increased market share is often billed as a healthy sign that news organizations are both independent and concerned with improving their news coverage. Rather than denigrate the press corps as a "pack," it is frequently claimed that individual reporters compete with one another for the freshest, most insightful angle on a story. Indeed, most of the defining characteristics of the professional press in America seem designed to reduce the chance that news bias will result from standard reporting practices. It is certainly worth asking the obvious question: "How is it possible that journalists consistently report such narrow political views when they are overwhelmingly committed to a professional code of independent, adversarial, objective reporting?" Any adequate explanation of political bias in the news must confront the problem of how such bias occurs in spite of strongly held professional values and practices that are widely regarded as insurance against it.

Not only do most reporters view the commitment to objective reporting as serious and credible,[19] but virtually every embattled politician since George Washington has accused the press of adversarial coverage. Even many members of the public seem convinced that the news, at worst, has a liberal, rather than an establishment, slant.[20] Nowhere in this popular scheme of things is there much room for the idea that the news marches in lockstep with powerful elites (both left and right) and non-threatening popular groups against the interests of large numbers of silenced Americans. Thus an adequate explanation of how the news comes by its status quo bias not only must explain the failure of professional norms to prevent such bias but also must account for the widespread belief of journalists, politicians, and the public that those professional safeguards have not failed.

The explanation proposed here confronts the paradox of objective journalism by showing that *the news is not biased in spite of, but precisely because of, the professional journalism standards intended to prevent bias.* The central idea is that the professional practices embodying journalism norms of independence and objectivity also create conditions that systematically favor the reporting of narrow, official perspectives. At the same time, the postures of independence and objectivity created by the use of these professional practices give off the impression that the resulting news is the best available representation of reality. In short, professional journalism standards introduce a distorted political perspective in the news yet legitimize that perspective as broad and realistic.

Professional Journalism and Its Standard Defense

The popular defense of objective reporting is that it prevents, or at least minimizes, political bias and distortion in the news. The key practices that have fallen under the protective cover of "objective journalism" include the following:[21]

1. The professional journalist assumes *the role of a politically neutral adversary*, critically examining all sides of an issue and thereby assuring the impartial coverage of the broadest range of important issues.

2. The journalist resists the temptation to discuss the seamy sensationalistic side of the news by *observing prevailing social standards of decency and good taste*.

3. The truthfulness and factuality of the news is guaranteed by *the use of documentary reporting practices* that permit reporters to transmit to the public only what they can observe or support with physical evidence.

4. News objectivity is reinforced further by *the use of a common or standardized format for packaging the news: the story*. Stories serve as an implicit check on news content by requiring reporters to gather all the facts (who, what, when, where, how, etc.) needed to construct a consistent and plausible account of an incident. Since stories are also the most common means of everyday communication about events, they enable the public to judge the consistency and plausibility of news accounts. Moreover, since the use of stories is a standard reporting practice, the public can make systematic comparisons among the coverage given to events by different news organizations.

5. The use of standardized methodology and reporting formats enables any reporter to cover any kind of story, thus separating reporters from personal bias vis-à-vis the subject matter of the news. The *practice of training reporters as generalists* (as opposed to specialists) also helps to separate the desired documentary reporting function of journalism from undesirable pedantic or interpretive tendencies in news reporting.[22]

6. The above practices are regulated and enforced by the important *practice of editorial review*, which serves as a check against violations of the practices and norms of the profession.

When describing the major practices that comprise objective reporting, it is difficult not to mention their normative purposes in the same breath. As the above list indicates, practices and normative purposes are so closely connected in everyday usage that it is tempting to think that the practices were, in fact, designed to implement normative goals. Indeed it is difficult to imagine any other function for adversarial roles or documentary reporting or standards of good taste than the simple "objectification" of the news. It is also difficult to think that these practices do not help in some way to accomplish their stated purposes. Even if the press does not always succeed in its normative mission, the clear adherence to these newsgathering practices would seem to imply that the news must be as fair and objective as it can be, given the political pressures under which it is gathered.

The Shady Origins of Objective Journalism

Despite the appeal of the idea that professional journalism practices are logical derivations of the norm of objective journalism, there is considerable evidence that the practices preceded the norm. Most modern journalism practices can be traced to economic and social conditions affecting the success of mass market news around the middle of the nineteenth century. The objectivity norm did not emerge until the turn of the century when established news organizations began to legitimate their product and their status with claims about professionalism.

In the early days of the American Republic, the news was anything but objective. Most newspapers were either funded by, or otherwise sympathetic to, particular political parties, interest organizations, or ideologies. Reporting involved the political interpretation of events. People bought a newspaper knowing what its political perspective was, and knowing that political events would be filtered through that perspective. In many respects, this is a sensible way to approach the news. If one knows the biases of a reporter, it is possible to control for them in interpreting his or her accounts of events. Moreover, if reporting is politically oriented, it becomes possible to look at the same event through different points of view, thereby taking into account various angles, emphases, and features of the event. Finally, since political events generally convey political messages, an overtly political reporting style is more likely to draw these messages out than to let them slide by unnoticed (with the risk that they might pass for broad, nonpartisan perspectives).

Their strong commitment to political analysis in news reporting notwithstanding, the early newspapers suffered economic limitations that made them unable to compete for large market shares as the nation and its communication system grew during the mid-1800s. The early papers were modest operations with small local readerships. As the country grew, a number of important changes affected the economics of the news business. For example, population began to shift to the cities, creating mass audiences for the news. The rapid expansion of the American territory during the nineteenth century created a need for the rapid and large-scale distribution of "national" news. Rapid breakthroughs in printing and communication technologies made possible the production of cheap mass media news that could be gathered in the morning on the East Coast and distributed by evening on the West Coast.

These and other patterns in the development of the nation produced dramatic changes in the news. By 1848, a group of newspapers made the first great step toward standardized news with the formation of the Associated Press.[24] The idea of pooling reporters and selling the same story to hundreds, and eventually thousands, of subscribing newspapers meant that the news had become a profitable mass market commodity. Of course, the broad marketability of the news meant that it had to be stripped of its overt political messages so that it would be appealing to news organizations of all political persuasions. In this fashion, "documentary reporting" was born. Moreover, the transmission of national news over the telegraph wires dictated a simplified, standardized reporting format— something that could convey a large amount of information in the most economical form. Thus the analytical essay rapidly gave way to the news story. The story was the perfect skeletal form for transmitting information over the "wires." The *Who, What, Where, When, Why* of an event made for economical transmission and easy reconstruction and embellishment on the other end. As the market for mass media news grew, the demand for reporters grew along with it. Whereas writing a persuasive political essay required considerable skill in the art of argumentation and the science of political analysis, virtually anyone could compose a story. After all, stories are the basic media of communication about events in the everyday social world. The use of stories also guaranteed that the news would be intelligible to the growing mass news audience.

In this manner, the overlapping effects of communication technology, economic development, and social change gave rise to large-scale news-gathering and news marketing organizations. Along with these organizations came a standardized set of reporting practices. As mentioned above, news services like the AP ushered in the documentary report. The use of wire transmission, along with untrained reporters, promoted the shift to the story form. The discovery that drama sold newspapers promoted the first adversarial reporting. Early mass media reporters were rather like agent provocateurs, stirring up controversy and conflict in order to generate dramatic material for their stories. As papers began to compete in the marketplace they also competed for the "scoop" and the "big story," further stimulating competition and adversarialism among reporters. As news bureaucracies grew in response to their economic success, editorial review practices emerged as expedient means of processing the huge flow of news. Standards of good taste guaranteed the inoffensiveness and mass marketability of the news product, particularly with the advent of a large, educated, middle-class news audience toward the turn of the century.

Nowhere in this history of the development of modern journalism was there a guiding professional rationale for what was happening. Even though we tend to think of the practices that emerged from this period as the hallmarks of "objective journalism," the concept of "objectivity" and its related professional rationale came much later. Journalism, like most professions, developed a set of business practices first, then endowed those practices with a set of impressive professional rationalizations, and finally proceeded to rewrite its history in ways that made the practices seem to emerge, as if through immaculate conception, from an inspiring set of professional ideals.

In fact, the creation of a professional creed of "objective journalism" (and its use to describe existing reporting practices) can be attributed to a number of rather mundane causes. For example, successive generations of reporters began to regard their work as a skilled occupation that should demand higher status and better wages. The move toward a professional status both enhanced the social image of reporting and paved the way for higher wages by restricting the entry of newcomers "off the street" into the journalism ranks. Professionalism meant that formal training and screening could be required for skills that had been acquired formerly "on the job."[25] The image of professional reporting was advanced further by a group of big-city newspapers that sought to sell the news to the rapidly growing and untapped middle-class market at the turn of the century. Life in urban settings was becoming dominated by the affluent middle class of professional, clerical, and business people who sported formal educations along with intellectual pretensions. Representing the news as objective, nonpartisan, and tasteful became an effective marketing ploy geared to the life style of this group. Consider, for example, the *New York Times*' early slogans: "All the News That's Fit to Print" and "It Will Not Soil the Breakfast Cloth."[26] Thus, existing practices became redefined around a professional image that dressed old news content in a new style. This emerging professional image of the mainstream mass media also became a convenient means of discrediting the muckrakers on the journalistic left, and the sensationalistic "scandal sheets" on the political right.[27]

A final boost to the emerging code of objective journalism came in the form of a growing concern among intellectuals following World War I that democracy was in trouble and could be saved only by a professional press dedicated to the mission of providing objective information to the public.[28] This noble purpose helped consolidate the existing pressures for professionalization. Led by persuasive spokesmen like Walter Lippmann,[29] journalists began to regard objective reporting as both a description of their existing work practices and as a high moral imperative. Perhaps the best capsule summary of this curious transition of journalism from a business into a profession is Lou Cannon's observation that what began "as a technique became a value."[30]

Professional Practices and News Distortion

Each of the defining elements of objective journalism makes a direct contribution to news bias. Despite the professional rhetoric of objectivity to the contrary, each component of news objectivity creates conditions favorable to the reporting of status quo news. This should not be surprising in view of the above capsule history of the news profession. All the basic practices that later became known as "objective journalism" were developed as efficient means of selling mass social and political values to a mass audience. As diverse political perspectives gradually disappeared from the news, or became discredited as not "objective," it became increasingly easy to convince people that the dominant mass media political perspective that remained was somehow objective. The logic of such a claim is simple: As one reality comes to dominate all others, it begins to seem that the dominant reality is objective. The absence of credible competition supports an artificial claim of objectivity. Unfortunately, this illusion of objectivity has been created by a set of journalist practices that actively promote status quo political perspectives, while drowning out competing views. The following discussion shows how each element of "objective journalism" actively promotes narrow political messages in the news.

The Adversarial Role of the Press

If the media were truly adversarial in their dealings with politicians, they would face a serious dilemma: The news could end up discrediting the institutions and values on which it depends for credibility. If officials and their positions were routinely attacked or held suspect by journalists, the media would have no source of "official acknowledgments." To a remarkable degree, the illusion of news objectivity is maintained through a combination of the narrow range of perspectives admitted into the news and the heavy reliance in official views to certify those perspectives as credible and valid. Adopting a true adversarial position would, as Tuchman argues, "dismantle the news net":

> Challenging the legitimacy of offices holding centralized information dismantles the news net. If all of officialdom is corrupt, all its facts and occurrences must be viewed as alleged facts and alleged occurrences. Accordingly, to fill the news columns and air time of the news product, news organizations would have to find an alternative and economical method of locating

occurrences and constituent facts acceptable as news. For example, if the institutions of everyday life are delegitimated, the facts tendered by the Bureau of Marriage Licenses would be suspect. One could no longer call the bureau to learn whether Robert Jones and Fay Smith had married. In sum, amassing mutually self-validating facts simultaneously accomplishes the doing of newswork and reconstitutes the everyday world of offices and factories, of politics and bureaucrats, of bus schedules and class rosters as historically given.[31]

It is equally true, of course, that the news would lose its image of objectivity if reporters openly catered to the propaganda interests of public officials and government institutions. If both genuine adversarialism and its complete absence would undermine the illusion of news objectivity, then there is an obvious implication: Any observable adversarial behavior on the part of the press should reveal itself more as a *posture* of antagonism than as a no-holds-barred approach to the content of the news. A ritualistic posture of antagonism between press and government would create the appearance of mutual independence without throwing open the content of the news to the serious coverage of a broad range of political perspectives. Such ritualistic posturing would dramatize the myths of a free press and an open government that have been important parts of the American image since the days of the Zenger trial and the fight over the Alien and Sedition Acts. It is in the nature of ritual to evoke such myths or beliefs without necessarily subjecting the principles involved to risk of challenge. Indeed, the preservation of beliefs in the face of threatening practical contradictions is a typical function of ritual.[32]

If the adversarial relationship is a ritual that both mystifies and legitimizes the reporting of narrow political messages, then the following sorts of characteristics should be observed: (1) the incidence of criticism and confrontation should occur regularly, as a matter of everyday reporting orientation, as opposed to more sporadically, for example, when there is some demonstrable reason to believe that a serious political question is at stake; (2) challenges and charges will tend to be aired selectively both by the press, who, for example, favor interelite confrontations, and by politicians, who typically ignore the attacks of "fringe elements"; and (3) charges against officials will be restricted to them personally and clearly separated from their institutions and offices. Such characteristics should pertain equally to routine news coverage (e.g., events on a reporter's "beat") and nonroutine coverage (e.g., crises and scandals).

Evidence that the adversarial relationship is a ritualistic aspect of routine reporting comes from Orr's seminal study of the presidential press conference.[33] Analyzing data from a sample of Kennedy, Johnson, and Nixon press conferences, Orr found that the proportion of hostile or critical questions was virtually constant across Presidents, conferences, issue categories, and political contexts.[34] Not only did the incidence of confrontational questions fall into a routine pattern, but nearly all hostile questions were personal in nature. Many of those personal questions signaled clear deference to office and institution. Moreover, questions that could have been phrased as strong political attacks generally contained open invitations to redefine the issue or dismiss the entire question. Based on these patterns, Orr concluded that the adversarial postures of press and President create a dramatic image of journalistic aggressiveness while communicating a subtle message of institutional deference.

Similar ritualistic elements have been observed in the reporting of less "routine" events like scandals and crises. Such investigative reporting has been a hallmark of adversarial journalism. Despite the claims of journalists to the contrary, a number of observers have argued that crises and scandals have become routine news events, complete with stock reporting formulas.[35] For example, Altheide and Snow analyzed news coverage of the Carter administration's Bert Lance scandal.[36] They concluded that the scandal was cast quickly into standard reporting formulas. These formulas were not only instrumental in creating the scandal but also obscured indications of the actual political significance and magnitude of the incident. The coverage damaged Carter personally, while issues of office and state were assiduously avoided. The overall impression from the intense media investigation was one of dramatic confrontation between press and establishment, yet nothing was reported that might have jeopardized the overriding interests of either the press or the establishment.

In both routine and investigative reporting, the adversarial relationship is a ritual that creates an image of no-holds-barred reporting while circumscribing actual news content in the process. The ritualistic elements built into specific news stories are reinforced by more general adversarial postures that transcend specific stories. For example, one indicator of the commitment of the press to adversarial displays is the format of virtually every news interview and interview program, from the stage settings that place press and politicians in confrontational poses, to the "tag team" question-and-answer formats, to tone of voice and terms of address. Elites also contribute to this enduring antagonism by routinely attacking the press as liberal, biased, and hostile. Such attacks frequently appear in elite publications and occupy the agendas of business, government, and journalism symposia.[37] Occasionally such charges are dramatized through formal political attacks, such as the ones during the McCarthy era and the Nixon administration. One analyst found the Nixon-Agnew attacks on the press so ritualized that he interpreted them in terms of ethological concepts of animal aggression and territorial defense.[38]

Just as the ritualized coverage of specific stories is limited in political content, so too are the general adversarial postures moderated by the mutual acknowledgment of each side's political legitimacy. Antagonistic postures would serve neither press nor politicians if they succeeded in undermining the institutions of press or government. Thus, reporters are ever at the ready with pronouncements that "the system worked"—the dramatic end note to the Watergate crisis. At the same time, the news never pronounces official judgment that "the system failed." Politicians, for their part, acknowledge the legitimacy of the press in numerous ways, such as holding routine briefing and conferences, including journalists in all official state occasions, and treating the media as a sort of partner in official attempts to communicate directly with the mass public (e.g., town meetings, phone-in programs, and fireside chats hosted by news reporters and anchor personalities).

Simply because the press and public officials strike a careful balance between surface conflict and underlying value consensus does not mean that there is active collusion at work. As with most rituals, news reporting requires genuine involvement of actors in their roles. Both public officials and journalists are personally involved in the conflict over the presentation of daily news information. Both sides have enough to gain and lose on a personal level to make the displays of aggression genuine.[39] Nevertheless, each side also stands to undermine its own legitimacy by attacking the other on fundamental value questions. Hence a stable symbiotic relationship has emerged in which adversarialism seems genuine without presenting a risk of opening up news content.[40]

Standards of Decency and Good Taste

When viewed through their normative justifications, standards of decency and taste seem designed to keep the reporter's attention focused on important issues and away from the seamy, sensationalistic aspects of political life. Only in cases where questionable behavior reflects on leadership qualities or respect for law will the media turn its eye to moral questions, as happened, for example, with the extensive news coverage of the "Chappaquiddick scandal" involving Ted Kennedy. Despite the apparent justification for this restraint in raising moral questions, standards of decency and good taste help to create distorted news.

The practical application of standards of good taste creates two paradoxes for news content. First, standards of taste have a bias in favor of precisely those mainstream, status quo values that the bulk of political propaganda promotes.[41] Moreover, the avoidance of offensive ideas and values removes from the public awareness many undesirable but true aspects of the real world. As a result, the definitions of, and the solutions for the problems in, the news may appeal artificially to the hopes of the middle-class public because of the successful moralizing of propagandists who create news events that reify the status quo.

The second paradox of standards of taste results from the fact that they ignore a key feature of politics. Politics is the primary social activity through which wildly divergent values and morals come together in struggles for dominance and legitimacy. The selective attention to preferred morals not only passively promotes the work of propagandists, as mentioned above, but it actively distorts the values and issues at stake in many situations. In this latter role, standards of taste may lead to overt censorship of some aspects of news events, thereby making journalists active agents in shaping the definitions of political situations.

The capacity of standards of taste to affect the definition of political events is illustrated by the news coverage surrounding a statement made by Agriculture Secretary Earl Butz during the 1976 presidential campaign. While flying between campaign appearances, Butz made a blatantly racist remark to a group of reporters. This remark was not only significant on its own merits, due to its appalling racist content, but it was also pertinent to the campaign because it was offered in response to a question about Republican election strategies. Although the statement contains offensive language of the sort not often found in scholarly writing (not to mention news stories), its political magnitude can be conveyed only by quoting it directly. When asked about the efforts of the Republican party to mobilize the black vote, Butz remarked that it was pointless to worry about the black vote because blacks were unconcerned about politics. He then summarized his view of the concerns of blacks as follows: "I'll tell you what coloreds want. It's three things: first, a tight pussy; second, loose shoes; and third, a warm place to shit."[42]

It is arguably in the public interest to publicize a racist remark uttered by a U.S. cabinet officer while campaigning for the President who appointed him. However, the professional press regarded Butz's offense to good taste as a higher consideration than his offense to political sensibilities. The pervasive commitment to the decency code was reflected in a simple piece of data. Not one major news outlet ran the Butz remark at the time it was made. Only when the statement was quoted later at the end of a rambling article on the campaign in the underground newspaper *Rolling Stone* was it necessary for the respectable press to acknowledge that the incident had in fact happened. Even when major press and broadcast outlets ran the story, they did not use the verbatim language. Only one major daily paper (the Madison, Wisconsin, *Capitol Times*) and no commercial broadcast outlets used the actual words. In defense of their use of inoffensive euphemisms in place of the real language, editors and news producers pronounced the litany of the decency code. An editor at the *New York Times* put it this way: "... we recognized that if we used this series of filthy obscenities then we'll probably use the next." The editor of the *Des Moines Register* said he found the remark so offensive and so atrocious that "I couldn't bring myself to give it to people with their breakfast." The editor of the *Washington Post* produced a tortured chain of logic leading to the conclusion that only if the President himself had uttered the remarks would he have printed them, but lesser officials did not merit such a violation of the journalism code.[43]

The point is that the impact of the statement was lost when euphemisms were substituted for the actual language. As a result, the Ford campaign was spared the painful embarrassment of one of those rare moments when it lapsed from its agenda of carefully staged and scripted performances.[44] Such moments ought to be the focus of serious news coverage because they are as close as the public ever comes to witnessing natural political events. It is unfortunate that these incidents are often sheathed by the press due to their sharp moral edges.[45]

Documentary Reporting Practices

Objective reporting is based on the overriding principles that journalists do not embellish their stories, advocate particular interpretations of ambiguous events, or otherwise "make up" the news. The guarantee behind these principles is the practice of documentary reporting. Reporters trained in the documentary method are disposed to report only the information that they have witnessed and only the facts that credible sources have confirmed. Although the goals of documentary reporting are hard to fault, the practice of the documentary method creates a trap for journalists confronted with staged political performances. Only in rare cases when performances are flawed, or when behind-the-scenes staging is revealed, can reporters document in good professional fashion what they know otherwise to be the case: that the news event in question was staged for propaganda purposes. Since, as Boorstin pointed out, pseudo-events contain their own self-supporting and self-fulfilling documentation, the documentary method highlights the very aspects of events that were designed to legitimize them and to blur the underlying reality of the situation.[46] The paradox of the documentary method is clear: The more perfectly an event is staged, the more documentable and hence reportable it becomes.

In response to this dilemma, news organizations have begun to expose some of these planned "media events."[47] However, the proportion of stories exposing media events is minuscule in relation to the high percentage of news based on media events. The result of this imbalance between reported and actual occurrences of staged events may be similar to the distorting effects of adversarialism. By exposing only a fraction of the political manipulation in the news, journalists may reassure the public that they are monitoring such manipulation and alerting the public when it occurs.

The Use of Stories as Standardized News Formats

Although the origins of the story form were primarily economic in nature, stories quickly became justified in terms of the norm of objective journalism. Stories can be represented as standardized and mechanical means of communicating information—a representation that gives journalists a claim to a universal methodology of objective reporting. The problem with this normative definition of the news story is that it is a very selective rendition of what storytelling is all about. As anyone who has ever told stories knows, the telling of a story requires choices to be made about what information to include, what words to assign to the included information, and how to tie together all the chosen symbols into a coherent whole. These choices in turn depend on assessing the audience, the point that is to be made to that audience, and the plot techniques (flashbacks, sequencing, character development, climax, etc.) that will best make that point. In short, stories are not mirrors of events.[48] A well-constructed story may be plausible, but plausibility and truth in the world of storytelling have little connection.[49] An obvious implication of these features of storytelling is that they give reporters room to emphasize dramatic and literary aspects of events.[50] Epstein suggests that the use of artistic (i.e., literary, dramatic) forms in news construction is encouraged by editors, one of whom even issued a memo containing formal instructions about how to incorporate dramatic structure into stories.[51] Gans notes the frequency with which reporters "restage" aspects of stories to heighten their dramatic qualities.[52]

Despite the dramatic license offered by the use of stories, the wholesale invention of news plots would create enormous strains on the norm of objective reporting. One solution to this tension between the value of dramatic news and the commitment to documentary reporting involves the receptivity of news organizations to events that are staged dramatically by news sources. Even though these events are designed to convey loaded political messages, they do conform in a narrow sense to the norms associated with documentary reporting and story formats. So important is the dramatic element in political performances that they are often judged for newsworthiness on this criterion. Gans observed that "... an exciting story boosts morale; and when there is a long drought of exciting stories, they (reporters) become restless. In the Spring of 1978, some magazine writers, left 'crabby' by a drought of dramatic domestic news, joked about their readiness to be more critical of the President and other public officials for their failure to supply news that would 'make adrenalin flow.'"[53]

The use of stories also places another constraint on news content by promoting the use of standardized plots in news reporting. Any communication network based on stories will become biased toward particular themes. For example, criminal trials are dominated by such familiar plots as "mistaken identity," "victim of circumstances," and other plots that are relevant to the legal judgment of cases.[54] Storytelling between friends frequently centers on recurring themes that define the relationship and express the identities that the individuals have created in it. In politics, consensus and legitimacy can be promoted through the frequent and plausible use of the dominant values, beliefs, and myths of the political culture.[55] It is common knowledge that elites, leaders, and interest groups define political situations in the familiar themes of political culture. These themes, if used repeatedly, strike journalists and ordinary citizens alike as suitable framings of events. Gans has noted the domination of the news by a remarkably small number of recurring themes. These plot devices include "ethnocentrism" (America first, America-the-generous, America-the-embattled, etc.), "altruistic democracy," "responsible capitalism," and "individualism," among others.[56]

Political performances scripted around routinized themes legitimize the status quo and severely limit the range of political discourse.[57] However, reporters who are locked into the "formula story syndrome" are forced to invert the relationship between stories and reality so that formula stories become viewed as exhaustive representations of reality. This naive approach to objectivity gives news writing a mystical quality described by Darnton: "Big stories develop in special patterns and have an archaic flavor, as if they were metamorphoses or *Ur*-stories that have been lost in the depths of time. ... News writing is heavily influenced by stereotypes and by preconceptions of what 'the story' should be. Without pre-established categories of what constitutes 'news,' it is impossible to sort out experience."[58]

Not only do stories lock in the narrow political messages of routine news events, but the professional commitment to the news story can introduce equally serious distortion into investigative reporting. Stories, by definition, encapsulate events, making them seem to be self-contained and independent of external forces. Since the stories and tips provided to investigative reporters are often (one suspects, usually) motivated by political considerations on the part of the source, it is possible to frame the information given to reporters in ways that keep the political concerns of the source out of the picture. For example, Epstein has argued that the Watergate story based on the investigative reporting of Woodward and

Bernstein may have been only part of a much larger political scandal.[59] He argued that the source of the inside information necessary to keep the story unfolding seemed to provide only information which would turn the story toward the Oval Office. Epstein noted that there might have been other political actors, like the CIA, who could have been caught up in the Watergate scandal, and who would have benefited enormously by trying to encapsulate the issues in a story centered on the President and his men.

We will, of course, never know who set Nixon up for the story that emerged in the Watergate case. The point here does not depend on knowing who did it. In fact, the point is underscored by the fact that the reporting practices involved make it *impossible* to find out who did it or why. The obvious need to protect the confidentiality of sources is not the only, nor even the most important, reason why the political contexts of news stories are seldom disclosed. The elevation of the story form to a professional practice places an even more subtle prohibition on revealing the politics behind political news. There exists a fundamental contradiction between the pragmatics of story writing and the normative justification for the practice. The normative defense of stories is that they do in fact constitute complete and objective versions of events. It would be devastating to this simplistic view of news reality to show that behind every story lies another story that comes much closer to revealing the true politics of the situation. As Epstein explained, the story-behind-the-story approach to news reporting would blow the cover off the normative claim that objective reality can be encapsulated somehow in stories.

Reporters as Generalists

Stories play another role in journalism by representing a universal reporting "methodology" employed by all reporters whether they are reporters of politics, sports, or business. Reporters are trained as generalists who are able to write stories on any subject. Although a small percentage end up reporting in specialized areas like science or fashion, the majority change beats periodically and pride themselves on their ability to cover any news story.[60]

The emphasis in the profession on training reporters as generalists has obvious origins and payoffs. As Gans noted, "... the news is still gathered mostly by generalists. One reason is economic, for general reporters earn less and are more productive. Beat reporters can rarely produce more than one story per television program or magazine issue, while general reporters can be asked, when necessary, to complete two or more assignments within the same period."[61] Despite these obvious economic advantages, generalism is justified almost exclusively in normative terms. A key element of the journalism code is public service. The news is billed normatively as a democratic service to the mass public. The use of generalists who employ a standardized story format is justified as the best means of presenting comprehensible information to the average person. If a reporter has any special expertise on a topic, he or she may run the risk of complicating a story, or violating the story form altogether by lapsing into technical analysis. Whether or not there is any foundation to the belief that the general public cannot follow news produced by overly specialized reporters, this belief is widely shared by editors and producers in the news business. For example, Epstein reported the following response of an NBC news executive to a Justice Department suggestion that the television networks use correspondents with special knowledge of ghetto problems to cover urban riots: "Any good journalist should be able to cover a riot in an unfamiliar setting.... A veneer of knowledgeability in a situation like this could be less than useless."[62] In another case Gans reports a comment by an executive producer to his economic reporter following a good story on a complicated subject: "You scare me with your information; I think we'll put you on another beat."[63] Gans also noted the general anxiety shared by many specialists that they were becoming too knowledgeable for the likes of their audiences or their superiors.

Although generalism is justified normatively as a necessary concession to a mass audience, the audience may pay a high political price in exchange for the alleged gains in news comprehension. Generalist reporters are often at the mercy of the news source. In technical areas generalists are seldom qualified to ask critical questions.[64] As a result, reporters may have to ask news sources for guidelines about appropriate questions. Even when generalists are assigned to fairly straightforward political stories, they may have to fashion their stories almost entirely from official pronouncements and the story angles pursued by other reporters.[65] As a result of greater dependency of generalists on their sources, the odds are even greater that they will report fabricated events. Moreover, generalists may be less likely than specialists to spot flaws in performances that would make it possible to expose the contrived nature of an event. For example, Gans noted of generalists: "Not knowing their sources well enough to discount self-serving information, they may report an opinion or a hopeful guess—for example, the size of an organization's membership—as a statistical fact. In this way, enterprising politicians sometimes get inflated estimates of their support into the news. ... Occasionally, general reporters may cover only one side of a story without ever knowing that there are other sides."[66] Thus generalism, like other reporting practices, is justified as a public service, but in fact it increases the likelihood of elite control of the news.

The Practice of Editorial Review

It is hard to imagine a criticism that could be lodged against the journalistic commitment to editorial review. The review policies of most news organizations are represented as insurance that the professional practices discussed above will be used in reporting the news. In a sense, editorial review does serve this function, thereby ensuring the news distortion produced by these journalistic practices. Editorial review also exerts its own influence on the political content of the news. Editors are not just the overseers of news production; they are accountable to management for the competitive market position of their news product. As a result of this accountability, editors and owners (or managers) typically formulate implicit criteria that their news product must satisfy in order to be successful and professionally respectable in their eyes. Studies of the internal workings of news organizations make it clear that these implicit criteria are major factors in socializing reporters and shaping the political content of news.[67]

These implicit editorial criteria would not be a problem if they were idiosyncratic. However, news organizations are businesses driven by the same economic imperative that exists in any large market dominated by a small number of competitors. This imperative, as noted earlier, is the same whether applied to political campaigning in a two-party system, news reporting in a three-network market, or car production in a three-company industry: Standardize the product as much as possible so as to minimize the risk of losing a minimally acceptable share of the market, and compete for greater market share via production efficiencies and market techniques. The consequence of this imperative for the news is twofold. First, most editors find it expedient to take their story leads from the wire services. The reliance on the wire services as implicit standardizing mechanisms applies both to print and broadcast media.[68] Second, editors tend to standardize their product further by bringing it in line with the competition. Due to the conservative imperatives in news production, it is easier to justify similarities in the coverage of stories than to account for differences between organizations. To put it simply, the transparency of the "objectivity" claim becomes most evident when the coverage of one organization differs from the others and must, as a result, be defended against queries by publishers, politicians, and the public. The best defense of objectivity is contained in the implicit standardization of editorial review practices.

The obvious political consequence of standardized editorial policies was captured nicely by Diamond, who noted that editorial practices reinforce the worst tendency in the news business to stereotype stories. News stereotypes conform to the major plot outlines of fabricated news performances and give the news its obvious status quo bias. As Diamond notes, none of this bias can be attributed directly to political motives on the part of reporters. To the contrary, the professional standards of journalists cleanse the news of such motives; yet, somehow, the resulting product does seem to display a particular slant: "The press isn't 'racist,' though as the skins of the participants become darker, the lengths of the stories shrink. The press isn't 'pro-Israeli,' though it is very sensitive to Jewish-American feelings. The press isn't afraid of the 'vested interests,' though it makes sure Mobil's or Senator Scott's denials appear right along with the charges. The paranoids are wrong: there is no news conspiracy. Instead there are a lot of editors and executives making decisions about what is 'the news' while constrained by lack of time, space, money, talent, and understanding, from doing the difficult and/or hidden stories."[69] In short, the editorial review standards pointed to as the fail-safe mechanism for preventing news distortion are, paradoxically, the very things that guarantee news distortion in the final analysis.

Objectivity Reconsidered

It is clear that the news does not hold up very well under scrutiny of the normative claims made about it. A number of observers have argued persuasively that whatever the news is, it is not a spontaneous and objective mirror of the world. Nevertheless, it would be a mistake to draw from the contradiction between journalism norms and practices the conclusion that neither the objectivity norm nor the reporting practices matter. The objectivity norm hides the connection between reporting practices and their economic, organizational, and political contexts. At the same time, the objectivity norm gives the press the look of an independent social institution. Moreover, even though actual reporting practices distort the political content of the news, they fit conveniently into the objectivity code, thereby obscuring their political effects. In this fashion, journalistic norms and reporting practices operate together to create a strong status quo bias in the news—a bias that is well hidden behind a facade of independent journalism.

Notes

1. See, for example, the numerous accounts of reporters, including Lou Cannon, *Reporting: An Inside View* (Sacramento: California Journal Press, 1977); Robert Darnton, "Writing News and Telling Stories," *Daedalus* 104 (Spring

1975): 175–94; and Lewis Lapham, "Gilding the News," *Harper's*, July 1981, pp. 31–39.

2. For an excellent discussion of this syndrome, see Gaye Tuchman, *Making News: A study in the Construction of Reality* (New York: Free Press, 1978).

3. For a detailed analysis of how this pattern occurs, see Leon Sigal, *Reporters and Officials* (Lexington, Mass.: Heath, 1973).

4. Tom Bethell, "The Myth of An Adversary Press," *Harper's*, January 1977, p. 36.

5. Quoted in David Owen, "The Best Kept Secret in American Journalism is Murray Kempton," *Esquire*, March 1982, p. 50.

6. See, for example, Warren Breed's classic study, "Social Control in the Newsroom," *Social Forces* 33 (May 1955): 326–35.

7. Edward Jay Epstein, *News from Nowhere* (New York: Vintage, 1973).

8. Ibid.

9. These observations and hypothetical examples are reconstructed from discussions with members of marketing and news production staffs in news organizations that have hired the services of news consultants. For obvious reasons, these people wish to remain anonymous. The reader can read more about the news doctors by consulting the running dialogue about them that has emerged in publications such as the *Journal of Broadcasting* and the *Columbia Journalism Review*.

10. Ben H. Bagdikian, "Fat Newspapers and Slim Coverage," *Columbia Journalism Review*, September/October 1973, pp. 17–19.

11. Fred C. Shapiro, "Shrinking the News," *Columbia Journalism Review*, November/December 1976, pp. 23–24.

12. Fergus M. Bordewich, "Supermarketing the Newspaper," *Columbia Journalism Review*, September/October 1977, p. 27.

13. Quoted in ibid., p. 25.

14. See, for example, Philip Meyer's criticism of marketing research and defense of more reliable social science investigations in his article, "In Defense of the Marketing Approach," *Columbia Journalism Review*, January/February 1978, p. 61.

15. See Timothy Crouse, *The Boys on the Bus* (New York: Ballantine, 1973).

16. Mark Fishman, *Manufacturing the News* (Austin: University of Texas Press, 1980), pp. 80–81.

17. Ibid., p. 81.

18. Stephen Hess, *The Washington Reporters* (Washington, D.C.: Brookings Institution, 1981), p. 130.

19. John W. C., Johnstone, Edward J. Slawski, and William W. Bowman, *The News People: A Sociological Portrait of American Journalists and Their Work* (Urbana: University of Illinois Press, 1976). Also: Charles J. Brown, Trevor R. Brown, and William L. Rivers, *The Media and People* (New York: Holt, Rinehart and Winston, 1978); and Hess, *Washington Reporters*.

20. See, for example, Edith Efron, *The News Twisters* (Los Angeles: Nash, 1971); and Doris Graber, *Mass Media and American Politics* (Washington, D.C.: Congressional Quarterly Press, 1980), Chap. 10.

21. For a review of these professional norms, see John Tebbell, *The Media in America* (New York: Mentor, 1974); Johnstone, Slawski, and Bowman, *The News People*; Tuchman, *Making News*; and Michael Schudson, *Discovering the News: A Social History of American Newspapers* (New York: Basic Books, 1978).

22. In recent years, the much-touted specialist has entered the reporting ranks. However, the use of specialists continues to be restricted to a few subject areas like science and economics. Also, specialists are employed by a relatively small number of big news organizations. Since the bulk of political reporting continues to be done by generalists who rotate assignments periodically and who refrain from introducing technical or theoretical perspectives in their reports, the practice of generalism merits inclusion here.

23. For supporting evidence for this claim, see, among others, Meyer Berger, *The Story of the New York Times* (New York: Simon and Schuster, 1951); Frank L. Mott, *The News in America* (Cambridge, Mass.: Harvard University Press, 1952); Edwin Emery and Henry Ladd Smith, *The Press in America* (New York: Prentice-Hall, 1954); Tebbell, *Media in America*; and Schudson, *Discovering the News*.

24. For discussions of the origins and impact of the wire services, see Bernard Roscho, *Newsmaking* (Chicago, University of Chicago Press, 1975); Mott, *News in America*; and Emery and Smith, *Press in America*.

25. Tebbell, *Media in America*.

26. Schudson, *Discovering the News*.

27. Upton Sinclair, *The Brass Check* (Pasadena, Calif: Published by the Author, 1920). Also, Berger, *Story of the New York Times*; and Tebbell, *Media in America*.

28. For a history of this period and its ideas, see, among others, Harold J. Laski, "The Present Position of Representative Democracy," *American Political Science Review* 26 (August 1932): 629–41; John Diggins, *Mussolini and Fascism: The View from America* (Princeton: Princeton University Press, 1972); and Schudson, *Discovering the News*.

29. See the following books by Walter Lippmann: *Drift and Mastery* (New York: Kennerly, 1914); *Liberty and the News* (New York: Harcourt Brace, 1920); *Public Opinion* (New York: Free Press, 1922); *The Phantom Public* (New York: Harcourt Brace, 1925).

30. Cannon, *Reporting: An Inside View*, p. 35.

31. Tuchman, *Making News*, p. 87.

32. See, for example, Murray Edelman, *The Symbolic Uses of Politics* (Champagne-Urbana: University of Illinois Press, 1964); Peter L. Berger and Thomas Luckmann, *The Social Construction of Reality* (New York: Anchor Books, 1966); and W. Lance Bennett, *Public Opinion in American Politics* (New York: Harcourt Brace Jovanovich, 1980), chaps. 13, 14.

33. C. Jack Orr, "Reporters Confront the President: Sustaining a Counterpoised Situation," *Quarterly Journal of Speech* 66 (February 1980): 17–32.

34. Ibid., p. 22.

35. See, for example, Harvey Molotch and Marilyn Lester, "Accidents, Scandals, and Routines: Resources for Insurgent Methodology," *Insurgent Sociologist* 3

(1973): 1–11; Molotch and Lester, "News as Purposive Behavior: On the Strategic Use of Routine Events, Accidents, and Scandals," *American Sociological Review* 39 (February 1974): 101–12; Murray Edelman, *Political Language* (New York: Academic Press, 1977), chap. 3; Todd Gitlin, *The Whole World Is Watching* (Berkeley: University of California Press, 1980), Chaps. 2, 7; Graber, *Mass Media in American Politics*, chap. 8.

36. David L. Altheide, and Robert P. Snow, *Media Logic* (Beverly Hills: Sage, 1979), chaps. 3, 4.

37. See, for example, Howard Simmons and Joseph A. Califano, Jr., eds., *The Media and Business* (New York: Vintage, 1979).

38. Henry Beck, "Attentional Struggles and Silencing Strategies in a Human Political Conflict: The Case of the Vietnam Moratoria," in *The Structure of Social Attention: Ethological Studies*, ed., M. R. A. Chance and R. R. Larson (New York: Wiley, 1976).

39. It is not hard to understand why politicians often become personally embittered over their treatment by the press. Although it often seems that politicians adopt a "sour grapes" attitude about the adversarial norm itself, it is worth considering the validity of the politician's typical complaint that news coverage is arbitrary, gratuitous, and unpredictable. These may be reasonable perceptions of journalists' ritualistic behaviors.

40. It is worth considering the depth of overlapping constraints imposed by this ritual on news content. For example, politicians who are personally threatened by the arbitrary adversarialism of news coverage are likely to be even more guarded in their definition and presentation of public statements. Thus the ultimate paradox of adversarialism may be that it fuels what is already a major source of news distortion: the use of propaganda as the everyday medium of political communication. When politicians regard reporters (in a sense, correctly) as people who are out to get them, politicians may treat reporters, in turn, the way Lyndon Johnson did, as "people who had to be bamboozled, bullied, cajoled, or bribed with entertainment." Quoted in George E. Reedy, "The President and the Press: Struggle for Dominance," *The Annals* 427 (September 1976): 67.

41. See Jacques Ellul, *Propaganda* (New York: Vintage, 1973).

42. Quoted in *Rolling Stone*, 7 October 1976, p. 57.

43. For these and other editors' responses, see Priscilla S. Meyer, "Hello, Rolling Stone? What Did Butz say?" *Wall Street Journal*, 7 October 1976, p. 18.

44. When the national press finally acknowledged the incident, Ford had little choice but to fire Butz. However, one suspects that Butz's desire to exit the situation gracefully, and Ford's wish to minimize his political losses, could not have been satisfied any better than through the delicate treatment accorded to the episode by the journalistic community.

45. This moralism of the press makes less sense as an enhancer of news content than as a spinoff of the economic base of the media. As mentioned earlier, a key part of the market strategy of the turn-of-the-century press was to appeal to the moral sensibilities of the most affluent, rapidly growing, and untapped mass news market: the middle class. From these beginnings, the news has helped create a restricted picture of American society in two ways. First, by

representing the world through middle-class values, the news became an implicit model for social propriety. Second, by introducing selective moral perspectives into news coverage, the press tacitly became the legitimator of the same values it helped to promote.

The strength of middle-class moralism in the news business is formidable. For example, even a semisensationalist paper like the *New York Daily News* did not print the word "syphilis" until 1931. One suspects that the phenomenon to which this word refers was an important social problem long before the respectable reading public was exposed to it in print. Similarly, the prototype of the highbrow, family newspaper, the *New York Times*, refused to review Kinsey's landmark study of sexual behavior until it had been certified by the academic community, long after the publication date, as a serious scholarly work (see Tebbell, *Media in America*, p. 141). One also suspects that human sexual behavior was a significant and widely practiced phenomenon long before the *Times* endorsed it as a subject worthy of discussion.

46. Daniel Boorstin, *The Image* (New York: Atheneum, 1961).
47. See Edwin Diamond, *Good News, Bad News* (Cambridge, Mass.: MIT Press, 1978).
48. See W. Lance Bennett, "Storytelling in Criminal Trials: A Model of Social Judgment," *Quarterly Journal of Speech* 64 (February 1978): 1–22; and W. Lance Bennett and Martha S. Feldman, *Reconstructing Reality in the Courtroom* (New Brunswick, N.J.: Rutgers University Press, 1981).
49. Bennett and Feldman, *Reconstructing Reality in the Courtroom*, Chap. 4.
50. James David Barber, "Characters in the Campaign: The Literary Problem," in Barber, ed., *Race for the Presidency: The Media and the Nominating Process* (Englewood Cliffs, N.J.: Prentice-Hall, 1978).
51. Epstein, *News from Nowhere*, pp. 4–5.
52. Herbert Gans, *Deciding What's News* (New York: Vintage, 1979), p. 173.
53. Ibid., p. 171.
54. Bennett, "Storytelling in Criminal Trials," and Bennett and Feldman, *Reconstructing Reality in the Courtroom*.
55. See Murray Edelman, *Political Language* (New York Academic Press, 1977); and W. Lance Bennett, *Public Opinion in American Politics* (New York, Harcourt Brace Jovanovich, 1980).
56. Gans, *Deciding What's News*, Chap. 2.
57. See Tuchman, *Making News*; and Fishman, *Manufacturing the News*.
58. Robert Darnton, "Writing News and Telling Stories," *Daedalus* 104 (Spring 1975): p. 189.
59. Edward Jay Epstein, "The Grand Cover-Up," *Wall Street Journal*, 19 April 1976, p. 10.
60. Johnstone et al., *News People*.
61. Gans, *Deciding What's News*, p. 143.
62. Epstein, *News from Nowhere*, p. 137.
63. Gans, *Deciding What's News*, p. 143.
64. Ibid.
65. Ibid.; Also, Crouse, *Boys on the Bus*.
66. Gans, *Deciding What's News*, p. 142.

67. See, for example, Breed, "Social Control in the Newsroom;" Walter Geiber, "Across the Desk: A Study of 16 Telegraph Editors," *Journalism Quarterly* 33 (Fall 1956): 423–32; Epstein, *News from Nowhere*; Crouse, *Boys on the Bus*; and Gans, *Deciding What's News.*

68. For discussion of the impact of wire services on newspaper coverage, see: Crouse, *Boys on the Bus*; and Sigal, *Reporters and Officials*. The impact of the "wires" on television news is discussed extensively in Epstein, *News from Nowhere*; and Gans, *Deciding What's News.*

69. Diamond, *Good News, Bad News*, p. 228.

FOUR

The Public: Prisoners of the News

We're living in the future
Tell you how I know
I read it in the papers fifteen years ago.

JOHN PRYNE

It should be clear by now that the news is neither made nor reported primarily for the purpose of providing citizens with useful political information. Both politicians and journalists are concerned with more immediate goals than the problem of how to give people an accurate and useful picture of the world in which they live. As a result of the political and journalistic factors that shape the news, the public is placed in a difficult bind. On the one hand, those who pay serious attention to the news run the risk of absorbing its subtle political messages, accepting its familiar stereotypes, and adopting its rigid modes of thinking. On the other hand, people who avoid the news may suffer the social stigma of ignorance, the guilt of being poor citizens, and the confusion of not knowing what is happening in the world.

There are, of course, some people who seem to penetrate the screen of stereotypes and propaganda that dominate the news. Most of us have encountered people who can bring a news story into clear focus by adding a bit of background information or political analysis to the report. Since the news must be judged ultimately in terms of its political effects on the people who consume it, there are two important questions to be addressed at the outset of this chapter:

1. What enables a comparatively small number of people to make insightful and independent interpretations of the news?

2. Why do most people remain prisoners of the news, either forced to accept its simplistic political messages or resigned to a life of confusion about the world around them?

Escaping the News Prison: How People See Beyond the Walls

A small percentage of people stand in sharp contrast to the majority who absorb and expel news information as though they were contestants in a lifelong trivia match. Some people seem to have an inside line on the politics behind news reports. If, by this stage in the book, you are not such a person, at least you have all the information you need to figure out how these people come into the world.

Consider two facts that help explain who becomes liberated from the political confines of the news. First, we already know that the news consists overwhelmingly of "objective," "documentary" reports that pass along, with little analysis, the political messages of official spokespersons. As noted in Chapter 2, less than 1 percent of mass media coverage contains any sort of independent analysis from the reporter's perspective, while around 90 percent of the news originates from circumstances that give officials substantial control over political content. Second, consider the fact that most Americans who are politically active, system-supporting citizens have been socialized in environments (family, school, workplace) that discourage analytical or ideological political thinking. This combination of nonanalytical news with nonanalytical people does not bode well for much analytical thinking in response to political messages in the news.

A third factor further undermines the critical thinking of the public. As noted in Chapter 2, political actors tend to construct simplistic political messages that appeal to myths and unquestioned beliefs held by large segments of the public. Such messages are seldom brought into focus because of the absence of analysis in the news and the lack of analytical dispositions in the audience. As a result, most news messages appeal directly to unconscious myths and unquestioned beliefs. In short, the propagandistic, nonanalytical qualities of mass news mesh smoothly with the well-conditioned, nonanalytical orientation of the citizenry.

This profile of the news prisoner contains an obvious clue about those who escape. In order to escape the news prison, people must develop some independent, analytical perspective with which to interpret the news. So much for the obvious. The more difficult problem is to identify the sort of perspective that helps people understand the news more clearly. There are actually several orientations that would enable people to break through the layers of subtle persuasion in the news and think sensibly about what might be going on behind the stories. For example, a grasp of American history would provide a perspective on the patterns of myth and rhetoric in political events. A common technique of political propaganda is to blur the relationship between past and present. When historic disasters like foreign involvements or economic collapses seem to be on the verge of recurring, public officials can be expected to persuade the public that important differences distinguish present circumstances from the past. At other times, when the signs of change seem entirely clear, threatened elites may try to persuade the public to avoid the fearsome future and step back into the comforting shadow of the past. The repeated and successful use of these communication patterns suggests that the American people can be led easily to see differences where none exist and to ignore distinctions where they are apparent.

A firm grasp of political history would provide people with a more secure foundation than they now have from which to resist political pressures and with which to develop alternative understandings. Unfortunately, most school boards look with disfavor on history curricula that offer coherent interpretations of American politics. As a result, the majority of American children suffer through year after year of the same history course—a course that emphasizes disconnected facts and events, that reinforces basic myths that leave people vulnerable to political rhetoric, that discourages people from developing a secure understanding of power and politics in American society, and, above all, that emphasizes the deeds of great national heroes. This "hero history" not only brings myths to life, but also encourages people to trust contemporary hero-leaders to do their thinking and acting for them. There are, to put it bluntly, few Americans with an adequate grasp of their country's history.

Another possible frame of reference on the news would be the sort of perspective provided in this book, namely, a theoretical grasp of how politicians and journalists act together to make the news. Such a perspective would help people to locate and interpret the gaps and biases in mass media coverage. When diplomatic talks are called "cordial and productive," people could assume immediately that nothing had happened and that the leaders involved had some other political reason to hold the conference. People could recognize political manipulation in the news through the use of leaks, pseudoevents, and various image-making techniques. After hearing "both sides of an issue," people might even begin to wonder what the third side looked like and why it was not reported.

Unfortunately, people are not required to take courses on how to interpret the news. To the contrary, most people are encouraged by every trusted authority, particularly parents and teachers, to take the news seriously, at face value. The majority of us are taught to ingest large quantities of news and wait for an objective understanding of events to strike as if by revelation. Waiting for objective revelations from the news may be more satisfying than waiting for Godot, but it is surely as pointless. Children are quizzed in school on the content of *My Weekly Reader* as though it represented the most accurate and comprehensive coverage of the known world. By memorizing the "right answers" to news quizzes, these children grow up thinking that knowing the facts in the news is equivalent to understanding something about the real world.

The news worship that begins in childhood is continued in adult life by the widespread support for the ideal of objective reporting. The notion that events can and should be presented without values or interpretation feeds the image of the good citizen as a concerned seeker of truth. At the same time, the widespread belief in objective reporting obscures the possibility that most "truths" that emerge from the news are likely to be the result of subtle political messages that appeal to subconscious beliefs and prejudices. People can hardly be blamed for thinking that they have found truth under such circumstances. After all, few things seem as objectively true as having one's deepest prejudices confirmed by respected authorities.

In the absence of a grasp of news theory or political history, the only other obvious source of independent news judgment is political ideology. Ideologies are formal systems of belief about the nature, origins, virtues, and means of promoting values that people regard as important. Not only do ideologies provide people with a clear sense of life's purpose, but they provide a logic for interpreting the world. Since ideologies refer to values that exist or should exist in the real world, they contain rules for translating real-world events into illustrations of how those values are promoted or damaged. Thus, people who view the news through the lens of an ideology are likely to spot hidden political messages and translate them into independent political statements.

It is true, of course, that ideologies can become rigid and limiting frames of reference, depending on how they are used. Yet it is hard to imagine circumstances under which they would be more limiting than the standard political messages that appear in the news every day. If used constructively, ideologies can create challenging understandings of the world by enabling people to find the inconsistencies, puzzles, and paradoxes in the events. Thinking through the puzzles in political events can broaden an ideology by adapting it to resolve the puzzles. This process of adaptation simultaneously creates new ways of seeing the world.

In a perfect world, people would supplement their ideologies with a command of history and a theoretical grasp of news politics. Such a combination of perspectives would enable people to combat news propaganda with their own grounded conclusions. This is not, as you probably guessed, a perfect world. It is unlikely that more than a tiny fraction of the public has an understanding of American history or news politics, and by even the most generous estimates, only 10 percent of the public can be called ideologues.

Even those few people who manage to construct a political world view may find it a mixed blessing. On the one hand, they are able to understand political communication in comprehensive and personally satisfying ways. On the other hand, their ideological insights are likely to be discredited by the majority of their fellow citizens, who have been taught to wait for "objective" revelations to emerge from the news. Hence, another paradox: People who espouse a stance of objectivity toward the news are likely to accept blindly the institutional bias of the mass media (if, indeed, they are able to form any political conclusions at all), while those who manage to form a clear political perspective are likely to be condemned for being "opinionated."

In order to understand the differences between the ways in which news prisoners and the relative handful of "escapees" react to the news, it will be helpful to explore the responses of some real people to a typical news report. The case study that follows involves an actual news story and the reactions it produced among members of a representative news audience. After thinking about this case, the reader might find it interesting to conduct a similar study to see if the results can be replicated.

The Case of the Killer Satellites

The example I have selected to illustrate the effects of familiar news messages on the average person comes from a study of political content in the news.[1] An initial sample of 2000 people was drawn at random from a commercial mailing list of the residents of a large (pop. 750,000) U.S. city. Such lists are used in marketing research and sales campaigns based on direct mail contact. Although commercial mailing lists are not perfectly representative of the general population, they tend to be distorted only at the very rich and very poor ends of the economic spectrum. The people included in this initial sample received an introductory letter from the *News Research Project* inviting them to participate in a detailed and somewhat time-consuming study of political attitudes and reactions to the news. A total of 375 people returned a preliminary screening questionnaire indicating that they had the combination of time, interest, and news contact required for participation in the study. These respondents were then sent a long, two-part questionnaire, the first part of which covered general attitudes about politics and journalism, while the second part asked for their reactions to actual news stories that appeared at the time of the study.

Participants were instructed to make contact with a particular news source on a specified day. The assignments of news sources (newspapers, television programs, magazines, radio, etc.) were based on each person's description of his or her news habits on the screening questionnaire. People were instructed to evaluate up to four stories of their choosing. The evaluation sheet provided for each story allowed participants to respond to the news in the following terms: (1) whether they learned anything new or useful from the report, (2) whether there was a message or a moral in the story, (3) whether there were actors in the story that produced positive or negative reactions, and (4) if anything reassured or disturbed them about the story.

A total of 268 people completed the questionnaires and news evaluations. The group broke down roughly along the lines of media use in the general population, with about half getting their news from television, one third using newspapers, 10 percent relying on radio, and the rest using news magazines or specialized publications. Since people were exposed to a variety of sources, for different lengths of time, and at different times of the day, there was some overlap and some divergence in exposure to the various stories of the day. The story about the "killer satellites" broke late in the day and appeared in the evening paper and on two of the network evening newscasts. Out of the estimated 75 people exposed to the story, 25 chose to evaluate it.

The killer satellite story had two equally dramatic plots. First, there was the revelation of a security leak by a member of Congress who was present at a closed-door briefing by a Defense Department expert. The congressman quoted from parts of the secret testimony at a subsequent open committee meeting. The second dramatic aspect of the story involved the topic of the secret briefing. According to the Defense expert, the Soviet Union had developed the capability to launch laser-equipped satellites that could destroy U.S. satellites and space stations. This science fiction motif prompted one of the television news programs to advertise its version of the story as follows: "Killer Satellites in Outer Space. . . . Coming Up Next."

All in all, it was a perfect news story with two great plots: a member of Congress on the hot seat, and a new twist on the arms race. The link between the two plots was provided by the Department of Defense, whose spokesperson said that it was "impossible to tell" how much damage had been done to the delicate U.S.-U.S.S.R. military balance by the leak of top intelligence information. The implication of the Defense Department statement was that the existence of laser satellites was bad enough but that letting the Russians know that we knew about them was even worse. An uneasy situation seemed to be complicated further by turning it into a public issue.

The security leak somehow added a sense of urgency to the latest twist on the old plot of conflict between the superpowers—if, indeed, the prospects of a war in outer space needed any embellishment. It is probably not surprising to learn that the overwhelming majority of those who evaluated this story indicated high levels of distress and concern about the arms race and U.S. military preparedness. People were able to respond to these thirty-year-old themes as though they had just encountered them for the first time. Not only does this response illustrate the power of news to continually breathe new life into familiar political messages, but it also illustrates the propensity for people to take political news seriously, at face value, even when there are many clues to suggest that propaganda is at work. Before exploring the actual responses of these "news prisoners" to the story, let's review the evidence for the possibility that the entire story was staged by government officials for propaganda purposes.

Consider some interesting facts that were available to anyone who had made contact with the killer satellite story in particular and the day's news in general. Any "news detective" should have found these facts puzzling:

1. The story originated with a Defense Department statement to the effect that it was impossible to tell how much "damage" had been done by the leak. If the Defense Department was afraid of whatever unspecified damage might follow from the leak, why did it go out of its way to issue such an inflammatory statement? Common sense would suggest a no-comment strategy, or an attempt to specify and minimize the possible damages, if, of course, the Defense Department had any interest in keeping the information secret.

2. The secret testimony was delivered at the time of crucial defense budget deliberations in Congress. The Defense Department typically offers such briefings in order to help members of Congress "understand" the true need for increased defense spending.

3. There was strong public resistance to the Defense Department's proposals for huge spending increases as the country was in the midst of a serious recession, and the defense increases would come in exchange for cuts in social programs.

4. The member of Congress read the secret testimony aloud at a public meeting. This is not the sort of anonymous release that usually accompanies leaks. Even though the representative claimed that reading the testimony was an accident, it is hard to imagine how anyone could quote directly from classified material without knowing what he was doing. Moreover, had the representative admitted to leaking the information on purpose,

he might have been subject to legal or ethics charges. All in all, it seems reasonable to suspect that he wanted the public to know about the latest Soviet military menace. Whether he leaked the information after consulting Defense Department officials is, of course, impossible to tell.

5. The only reporter present at the time the secret was leaked represented the *Army Times*. While it is true that the *Army Times* is not owned by the Defense Department, it is not clear that it is such an independent publication that it would have rejected the Defense Department's pleas not to publish secret information. A Defense spokesperson said that strong pressure was applied to the *Army Times*, but the paper published the story anyway.

6. If, as the Defense Department claimed, it wished to minimize the impact of the story, why did it then respond to the *Army Times* article by talking about "unknown damage" in U.S.-U.S.S.R. relations, and "impossible to assess" effects on the U.S. military posture? Such ominous comments escalated the story into a mass media news item the next day. Government officials generally refuse comment or issue statements minimizing the significance of events when they truly want to downplay a news story.

All of the above clues were available to everyone who read the story in question and who had even a passing familiarity with surrounding headlines proclaiming the political controversy over the proposed defense spending increases. The six clues, when put together, add up to an obvious conclusion about the story: The "leak" was a ploy to lend immediacy and credibility to standard Pentagon scare tactics designed to win public support for defense allocations every year around budget time. A second-party leak that is then condemned by the original source of the information makes the information seem all the more credible and compelling. When the Defense Department condemned the leak, it became hard to prove that they were simply playing budgetary politics with a new and rather deadly twist.

Even if caution would warn against leaping to conclusions, surely it would be hard to suppress doubts about the authenticity of this story! Unfortunately, most people are prisoners of the news who find it difficult to think analytically or critically about news events. As noted earlier, it is difficult to suspect ulterior motives on the part of public officials when we are taught to accept what authorities tell us. It is also hard to imagine that the news can be manipulated when we learn to accept it as a face-value rendering of reality. People may even be uncomfortable harboring suspicions about news manipulation when they cannot be proved conclusively.

Finally, it is difficult to make connections between news stories (e.g. linking the satellite story to stories on the defense budget) when most news reports are both fragmented and lacking in analysis. When all these factors are taken into account, it is perhaps disheartening, but hardly surprising, to find that most people took the killer satellite story at face value.

The overwhelming majority of people responded as though their lines had been scripted by the same authors who wrote the story. People were angered by the security leak, but this anger was overshadowed with genuine concern about the latest Soviet military advantage. A total of 25 people evaluated the story. Of these, 18 accepted, without question, the basic political messages of the story, while only 5 raised any questions about the honesty of the leak or the credibility of the message that "the Russians are ahead of us again." Two evaluations were too sketchy to be coded as either accepting or critical of the report.

Among the 18 people who accepted the report and its message without question there was not the slightest hint of doubt. These people were able to generate a remarkable degree of emotional distress about this latest episode in the U.S.-U.S.S.R. conflict. Even though the American people have been exposed to the same scare about Soviet domination over the past thirty years, it still seemed terribly real in its latest plot incarnation. Consider the following excerpts from the reactions of the 18 "believers" (their news sources for the story are in parentheses following their comments):

> Soviets will have space systems capable of attacking targets from space in less than 10 years. . . . We ought to be more concerned about Soviet capabilities. . . . People in responsible positions need to take extra precautions not to make public any secret testimony. (*Source: daily newspaper*)

> Testimony that was inadvertently made public implies that Soviets have a lead in development of killer satellites. . . . Peaceful purposes of U.S.-USSR space cooperation agreement seem far away. (*"NBC Nightly News"*)

> A leak of information by a Congressman of secrets relating to Soviet space weapons capable of destroying our (or any) other satellites. . . . Whole report disturbing. . . . Congressman who talked—DUMB! (*ABC*)

> USSR will have a laser satellite in space by next year, capable of destroying U.S. satellites with lasers. . . . The USSR is quite advanced in its space technology. . . . Having weapons in space disturbs me. (*NBC*)

> By 1983—Soviets will have laser-equipped space station. By 1990—Space station will be manned military operation. . . . Disturbing that a Congressman could "unwittingly" leak information by national security. (*ABC*)

> Russian arms in space can destroy U.S. satellites and land installations . . . . More care should be taken with the handling of secret information. (*ABC*)

> A general was shown advocating a U.S. system of 432 killer satellites. . . . U.S. may move into new arms race to build killer satellites, and despite

earlier Soviet-U.S. agreements on use of space for peaceful purposes—the reality may well be different. ... Idea of new arms race in space is most disturbing. (*NBC*)

The Soviets are apparently very interested in pursuing the military advantages of space technology. ... I'm concerned that the U.S.S.R. would use space for military purposes. I'm even more concerned that we will most likely follow suit with technologies of our own. (*newspaper*)

Defense Department scientist's secret testimony concerning Soviet laser weapons inadvertently leaked by Rep. Ken Kramer. ... The fact that the Soviet Union appears to be so far ahead of the U.S., and that Kramer's leak could be damaging to our national security—makes me tend to agree that defense spending is necessary, and wonder why more precautions aren't taken to preserve the confidentiality of such information. (*newspaper*)

Disturbing that the proliferation of new weapons continues with no apparent sign of abatement. (*newspaper*)

It was interesting to learn that laser beams could be used for this purpose. ... The build-up of arms for war is disturbing.(*NBC*)

We are behind in developing this technology. The disclosure came about on the public reading of classified information during a congressional investigation. ... The Soviet Union could orbit a laser weapon system that could strike at our orbiting communication satellites. (*newspaper*)

Geosynchronous satellites may be threatened by Soviet space-based lasers by 1983–88. ... How imminent such potential is I found extremely upsetting— the potential of such a manned space station is frightening to say the least. (*newspaper*)

There is evidence that the Soviets may have weapons in outer space. The Soviets seem to be ahead of us in outer space weaponry. (*ABC*)

A new dimension of warfare is coming of age. Facts were new to me. (*NBC*)

The Soviets are basically exploiting outer space as a platform for military operations. (*ABC*)

Some congressman leaked the information that the Soviets have a weapon satellite in space which can launch rockets at our satellites. By 1990 they will be able to launch a manned space craft with weapons to cover all earth targets. ... The message is that we are behind at this time regarding weapons in space. (*ABC*)

Russia is starting a weapon in space program and the American public found out because of a leak in Congress. ... I did not know before that anyone was working on a space weapon program but I always felt it would come about. (*ABC*)

As the above responses indicate, most people who evaluated the "killer satellite" story believed that the leak was an accident, and they expressed genuine alarm over the news that the Soviet Union was ahead of the U.S. in a new and deadly arms race. Only a small minority (20 percent) expressed any doubts about the sincerity of the story or the motives behind its message. It is also worth noting that only one of the skeptics had the strength of conviction that characterized all eighteen of the "true believers." As noted earlier, well-crafted propaganda does not provide the critic with much solid evidence to support doubts. Thus the voices of the doubters, already muffled by their small numbers, were weakened further by their tones of uncertainty:

> Russians may be ahead of us in space research. . . . Russians want to control space. . . . Are we really behind the Russians? Is this a controlled leak, i.e., set up by the U.S. government? (*ABC*)

> ". . . . the arms race is getting completely out of control. . . . I also wondered if the leak was an intentional scare tactic.(*newspaper*)

> The Soviet Union is ahead of the U.S., in satellite weapons. . . . Rep. Ken Kramer, the committee member who read aloud the secret testimony, is either incredibly stupid or is deliberately trying to arouse fear in U.S. public. . . . It is disturbing to be given a small bit of information without other confirmation or refutation. (*newspaper*)

> Nothing remains a secret in Washington, D.C., if somebody wants it leaked. . . . The D.O.D. is still up to their old game of trying to terrify Congress with the worst threat that the Soviets may (someday) be capable of mounting. I imagine the D.O.D. is not unhappy the leak happened; it will tend to help them in their budget battles in Congress. (*newspaper*)

> Was it a "slip" in having the story come out, or was it a planned "leak" to help continuing increased defense (budget) spending? (*newspaper*)

These responses indicate that not only are those who spot possible deception in the news few in number but they are less assertive than those who accept news messages without question. It may be that the sheer ambiguity that accompanies suspicions about news messages is unpleasant enough to turn doubters into believers. Although it is hard to tell precisely what separates the doubters from the believers, several features of the group profiles are worth noting. For example, the two groups did not differ in terms of the left-right leaning of their political views. The average person in both groups described his or her political views as "moderate." Neither was there much difference between the groups in terms of political activities, although the believers tended to be somewhat more active politically than the doubters. Believers felt slightly less able to change things that bothered them in their personal lives than doubters did, but the difference was not significant statistically. An interesting, but not easily interpretable, difference between the two groups involved the much higher levels of life stress reported by the doubters. Perhaps being a doubter is inherently more stressful than being a believer, or perhaps higher-stress people tend to be more critical of information in their environments than do low-stress people, or maybe stress is produced by the feeling that the government is lying to you and nobody else sees it that way.

Fortunately, we do not have to untangle the mysterious web of stress differences in order to identify an obvious distinction between the believers and the doubters. The two groups differ along two very fundamental dimensions. First, the believers reported that they were exposed to half again more news every week than the doubters reported! To be exact, news contact averaged 8.83 hours per week for the believers and only 5.20 hours per week for the doubters. Causality probably runs in both directions here, with people who find the news credible consuming more of it, while increased news contact reinforces the tendency to accept news messages at face value. Second, it is worth noting that 80 percent of the doubters read the story in the newspaper, while 67 percent of the believers watched the story on television. Not only may the amount of news contact affect the propensity to believe political messages, but the form of news contact may be important as well. Television is far and away the most popular news source, with nearly twice as many followers as the nearest rival, the newspaper. People claim to watch television news because they find it more credible or believable. For some reason, people think they are less likely to be fooled by a news report that they can see with their own eyes. It would seem that people have fooled themselves by adopting this "seeing is believing" attitude about televised news. Televised news stories may seem more credible because they contain pictures, or because they are more dramatic and absorbing, or merely because the actors in them make more of a semblance of human contact with the viewer. Far from being true indicators of truth, these features of television would seem to undermine basic human judgment. Television news may seem more objective, not because it enables people to judge stories better for themselves, but because it inhibits their judgment!

Whatever the differences between the believers and the doubters, one thing is clear: A dominant effect of the news is to continually dress old political messages in new story plots. Since the news is so vulnerable to political manipulation, the ulterior purposes and origins behind the ongoing stream of new stories and plot twists are seldom exposed. As a result, the majority of the people exposed to political messages in the news are likely to take them seriously and respond with the appropriate expressions of alarm, reassurance, activity or passivity in the political arena.

Is That All There Is? Other Reasons Why People Follow the News

The reassurance of hearing familiar messages and the comfort of having basic beliefs reinforced are both important reasons why people may follow the news. There are also other news effects that are worth knowing about. As noted in Chapter 1, news is a rich symbolic medium. Events are presented in dramatic terms with an emphasis on emotional themes and the exploits of a colorful cast of heroes, villains, prophets, and fools. Such rich symbolic content in communication lends itself to multiple human uses that go far beyond the simple quest for information. People also may receive a broad range of rewards or "gratifications" from such communication, gratifications that far outweigh the occasional satisfaction of using news information to make political choices and life decisions.

Research on the various "uses and gratifications" associated with the news can be summarized under three broad categories:[2]

1. *Curiosity and Surveillance.* Even though the political messages in the news are fairly predictable, the events, plots, and characters are constantly changing. Human curiosity is engaged by new events and novel twists on old themes. Moreover, some of the events in the news may have an impact on the people who follow them. Thus, many people find it useful to scan the news just to keep potentially important events under surveillance.

2. *Entertainment and Escape.* It is easy to become engaged by the drama of news events. The news makes everyday happenings seem larger than life. Most news reports invite us to escape for a minute or two into a story world filled with pathos, tragedy, moral lessons, crisis, mystery, danger, and occasional whimsy. The escape into this dramatic world is made all the easier when the happenings involve people like us, or people about whom we have strong positive or negative feelings.

3. *Social and Psychological Adjustment.* The emphasis on drama, emotional themes, powerful images, and strong personalities makes the news a convenient medium for working out psychological tensions and social conflicts. People do not even have to leave their living rooms in order to encounter real people about whom they have strong feelings, and issues that seem to affect their well being. By making connections between personal concerns and the events and personalities in the news, people can express feelings and think about their problems in uninhibited and often satisfying ways. This vicarious resolution of social and psychological strains is all the more effective because the realities of news stories are usually too distant for people to experience directly—thus the feelings and understandings people develop in response to the news are seldom subjected to reality testing.

Since all these uses and gratifications have important personal and political consequences, they are worth exploring in more detail.

Curiosity and Surveillance

People are blessed with curiosity—both as a source of sheer pleasure or amusement and as a means of spotting new information that might be useful in coping with everyday reality. Research has shown that our curiosity is peaked by things (e.g., situations, ideas, scenery, films, art, and news) that contain a mixture of familiar and novel features.[3] It is not surprising that human curiosity requires a combination of new and old stimuli in order to be satisfied. On the one hand, the repeated exposure to completely familiar stimuli results in the formation of subconscious mental "scripts" that make it possible to respond to situations without really thinking about them.[4] Curiosity and attention are minimized in such "scripted" situations. On the other hand, stimuli that are completely foreign may be so dissonant and hard to assimilate that people tend to ignore, avoid, or misinterpret them.[5] Partially familiar stimuli, by contrast, enable people to utilize existing mental categories and understandings and at the same time provoke people to modify or change those categories to accommodate anything that is new, different, or slightly out of focus.

News is the perfect blend of the familiar and the novel. The basic political messages in the news remain much the same, but they often appear in new settings and under different circumstances. There is an intrinsic satisfaction that comes from seeing how a familiar theme will develop in a new plot or whether an old plot will develop a new twist. For example, how will "freedom of choice"—a theme familiar to every American—be adapted to fit comfortably into such contexts as abortion, drug use, pornography, or the regulation of cigarette smoking in public places? Will the tired old plot of confrontation between the United States and the Soviet Union end in impasse as usual, or will there be a new twist this time? Perhaps a breakthrough in nuclear arms control? Perhaps a misunderstanding that will lead to human extinction? As long as new events keep happening in the world (and the chances are pretty good that they will), people will be drawn to the news as a means of applying, testing, and adjusting their understandings about reality. However, the news may be a dangerous object of curiosity due to its often distorted images of reality. People who regard mass media news as a satisfying source of objective information may be led astray by their own curiosity. For example, if the news persists in portraying the problems of the Third World in terms of the virtues of "development" versus the stigma of "underdevelopment," the news audience may fail to see many of the problems associated with rapid economic development in Third World societies—problems like the destruction of culture, the growing dependence of poor countries on the economies of rich countries, the political problems that accompany economic growth in repressive regimes, and so forth. All these problems contribute to the political and economic instability of those Third World countries that have entered the seemingly endless process of "development."

Despite its limitations, the development metaphor is written into each chapter of the "development saga" by government officials and cooperative reporters. Thus the latest collapse of a one-crop economy in an African nation may be attributed to a failure to diversify in the world marketplace. The failure to diversify is, of course, a symptom of underdevelopment. Never mind that the one-crop economy was forced on the nation by a former colonial regime—and never mind that the country's economic weakness may have been compounded after colonialism by wealthy countries that exploit one-product economies even more capriciously than the colonial powers did. The development metaphor needs no explanations; underdevelopment is at once the cause and the effect of an ill-defined economic condition. The solution, of course, is "development." In the case of our hypothetical Third World country, it is easy to imagine a subsequent news story describing a "development plan" for the troubled country—perhaps a massive infusion of loan funds has been offered by the World Bank. The money will be used to develop foreign-sponsored economic projects in the country. Even though the conditions of such loans, combined with the chronic dependence of indebtedness, will probably produce further setbacks in development, the immediate story now has a happy ending. Curiosity has been aroused by a new crisis in the world economy, and curiosity has been satisfied by resolving that crisis in terms of a familiar political concept. All just part of a day's work in the news world.

As long as the news continues to employ familiar but misguided themes in portraying the real world, and as long as people attempt to satisfy their curiosity about the world through the vicarious medium of mass media news this syndrome of political misinformation disguised by psychological gratification will continue to exist. The fact that massive doses of misinformation can prove so satisfying is just a small indicator of the degree to which the news removes people from the actualities of politics.

Before the reader concludes that I have overstated the case here, let me offer a qualification. It goes without saying that the news is not all as remote from everyday experience as the coverage of Third World development problems probably is. Some stories may arouse curiosity simply because they contain information that is immediately relevant to people. Not all curiosity is for the sake of sheer amusement. Even though people have the capacity to be curious about very abstract things, few people can, if you will pardon the paraphrase, live by idle curiosity alone. The news is all the more satisfying when it contains periodic information that is directly relevant to people. The reactions to such reporting differ in two interesting ways from reactions to more abstract stories. First, people are more likely to think in action-oriented terms about personally relevant stories. The more distant world of political news often leaves people with little option but to exercise their beliefs in a purely private fashion. Second, people express much less confusion and displeasure about news stories that satisfy curiosity with information that can be applied to immediate life concerns. Consider, for example, some typical reactions to different kinds of news stories from the News Research Project.

One of the stories in the news at the time of the study was a report on the financial troubles faced by four major airlines. The report outlined the various consequences for travellers, employees, and the economy if the airlines went bankrupt. Such information would seem to be of interest to a broad range of people. As a sign of the relevance of the information, everyone who filled out an evaluation of the story was able to find some personal use for the information. The range of uses was quite broad. For example, some people were alerted to possible difficulties in future travel arrangements, as indicated by this person's reaction: "I was disturbed by the fact that the failure of several airlines could result in increased inconvenience in travel." People who had already made travel plans were moved by the report to take direct action, as this response explains: "I found the story disturbing, as I have plane reservations in the spring with one of the airlines that may go bankrupt, so I plan to check with my travel agent about possibly changing airlines." Others found even more intimate applications for the information in the story, as revealed in the following reactions:

> I found the story disturbing as I have a friend that's been employed for several years by another of the airlines mentioned . . . .
>
> Reassuring that I am employed by an airline that is doing very well. Their loss is our gain.

It is significant that the airline story did not lead anyone to question its relevance or newsworthiness. Stories that are less personally relevant, by contrast, produce less satisfaction, as indicated by the comparative absence of stated uses for the information and the increased level of complaints about newsworthiness. For example, one of the stories in the study involved an incident between Nancy Kissinger (wife of former Secretary of State Henry Kissinger) and a political demonstrator at an airport. The demonstrator had filed a lawsuit alleging that Mrs. Kissinger assaulted her. Mrs. Kissinger claimed that she was simply defending her husband against a terrible insult from the demonstrator. None of the participants in the study who evaluated the story was able to find a direct personal application for the information it contained. At best the responses reflected the sort of trivia that often results from idle curiosity:

> I learned a little about Nancy Kissinger's personality.
>
> I learned that Henry Kissinger had a heart operation.
>
> How easy it is for someone to sue another person.

Nearly half the respondents were unable to find even such abstract and impersonal angles on the story. Many questioned its newsworthiness:

> I did not feel that this article should appear on the front page of the newspaper.
>
> No, I didn't learn anything, and it didn't rate the front page, except for its eye-catching function as a sales aid—à la National Enquirer.
>
> I am angry at how people involved resorted to verbal and physical attacks, but more importantly, that the article was placed on the front page—I doubt if the article has much significance—other than sensationalism.

Most news falls somewhere between the airline story and the Nancy Kissinger saga in terms of personal relevance. Most political stories, for example, are regarded as legitimate news in the sense that people react emotionally to them and believe them to be important. Nevertheless, few political stories provoke the sort of action or behavior orientation that the airline story did. In fact, few stories about political issues and government activities contain any more food for action than the Kissinger story did. A case in point was the major political story on the day that participants in the News Research Project were instructed to follow the news. President Reagan was on a speaking tour around the country trying to drum up public support for his budget. Despite his campaign promises of a balanced budget, the proposed budget contained the largest deficit in history. Much of the deficit was the result of increased defense allocations. A major section of the speech contained frightening references to the likelihood of war if America's defenses were not strengthened. So gripping were these images that over half the people exposed to this story chose to comment on it. Nearly all the respondents expressed a strong emotional reaction to the talk about war, and most people stated their opinion about the President's claims. Despite these strong psychological reactions, there was a nearly universal absence of ideas about personal actions that might grow out of the information in the story. In fact, only one person mentioned an action in response to the story, and it was not a very realistic one at that: the possibility of quitting work in order to campaign full-time against the President and his dangerous ideas.

The news world, in short, is rich in emotional triggers yet poor in guidelines for actions that might provide meaningful outlets for those emotions. The citizen who centers his or her political life on the distant world of news politics is a citizen by political proxy—at best, registering support through public opinion polls for the various issues and leaders that have been served up on the political agenda. Media politics is vicarious politics.

Entertainment and Escape

Speaking of vicarious involvement in the news raises the obvious issue of news as a source of entertainment and easy escape from mundane concerns. The news world may represent itself as a matter of fact, but it is communicated to the public with all the trappings of fiction: short, intense scenes; literary rather than analytical treatments; the nearly uniform used the story form; and the emphasis placed on drama, emotional conflict, and larger-than-life characters. The news may portray real events, but it does so in ways that discourage analytical or instrumental uses for the information it carries.

The news is, in short, a perfect medium for escape. Each day's news menu offers a large supply of complete minidramas for our entertainment pleasure. We can step into these fascinating fantasies for a minute or two, experience a brief sense of other lives and other worlds, and move on to the next one. In one moment we are a member of a guerrilla band on maneuvers in El Salvador, the next minute we move in with the survivors of an earthquake in Iraq, suddenly we are transported into the nightmare of a bank robbery-murder that was captured on the bank's closed-circuit video system. At last, the string of high-tension episodes is broken by a commercial that gives us a chance to regain our bearings, grab a snack, and get ready for the next installment of our evening's journey into real-life adventure.

Vicarious involvement in the news is often even more compelling than more conventional forms of escape via drama and literature. News dramas, after all, are represented as real, serious, important, and worthy of everyone's attention. Fiction, by contrast, does not involve real spies, real robbers, or real earthquakes. Fiction can at times command our attention, but fiction seldom combines the mixture of intensity, universality of appeal, and realism that characterize the news. A best-selling novel may sell a million copies during its lengthy run on the best-seller list, while 80 million people may tune into the news on a single day.

The seriousness or realism of the news is, paradoxically, a key to understanding its power as an escape medium. The general acceptance of the news as factual, important, and objective makes it easy for people to give themselves over to serious involvement with it. Once this easy surrender has taken place, the individual is then swept away by images and ideas that are often both stranger and more dramatic than fiction. For example, few novels contain plot twists like the news story about a band of thieves posing as police officers who were forced by circumstances to try to arrest a group of policeman disguised as a gang of thieves. The real police were—you guessed it—on the trail of the thieves who were posing as police. If a novelist were to submit such a plot to a publisher, it probably would be rejected as incredible or unrealistic. When it becomes news, however, no plot is too incredible to be engrossing. All plots are credible by virtue of the very fact that they are news. Thus the issue of credibility or realism, a major obstacle to involvement in fiction, is transcended easily by stories in the news, no matter how bizarre they may be.

The fact that news stories are thought to represent real situations adds to their entertainment value in at least one other respect. When dramatic incidents involve real people—people who feel, suffer, think, and die—a direct bond of human sensibility is created with the audience. Whereas fiction writers struggle to create such bonds through words and imaginary actions, the news generates them routinely by simply recording dramatic excerpts from real lives. Thus, few novels or movies about the horrors of war can rival the routine nightly installments on Vietnam witnessed by the American people between 1965 and 1970. Fictional accounts of political power and intrigue may achieve a measure of credibility, but few can match the daily revelations about power and corruption in the White House that filled the news during the time of the Watergate scandal.

In fact, the news is so dramatic that it increasingly supplies the plot material for novels, films, and new entertainment forms like the "docudrama." Novels have been written about murders, robberies, hijackings, and kidnappings that first captured the popular imagination in the news. Journalistic treatments of terrorism, political corruption, military operations, and spy escapades have spawned movies by the score. Even the journalistic practices behind the news have inspired entertainment fare, as in the case of Woodward and Bernstein's literary and film versions of *All The President's Men*—a highly dramatized account of how the two daring reporters conducted their famous Watergate investigation.

With the action news format gaining in popularity among those who run mass media news, we can expect the news to move ever closer to the routine distillation of factualized fiction or, if you prefer, fictionalized fact. Such a trend will only enhance the news as an escape medium and further undermine its potential to serve as an anchor of reality in contemporary life.

As Walter Lippmann pointed out over fifty years ago, the world of politics, as viewed by the public, will always be somewhat dramatized and fictionalized.[6] Politicians who control the flow of information will attempt, whenever possible, to shape news to their advantage. However, when the media actively seek dramatized reality to feed to a receptive audience, the only check on the representation of political reality is removed. When politicians, press, and public all judge political performances more in terms of dramatic criteria than moral standards, the conscience of the polity will be lost. Politicians will be free to lie and deceive at will (for it will no longer be thought of as lying and deception), and if they are challenged, they need only muster appropriate dramatic display of oversight, regret, misunderstanding, or good intentions.

If people become slowly conditioned to judge political performances for dramatic qualities rather than other features like truth, principle, or observable consequences, minor annoyances like inconsistency, duplicity, or failure on the part of the political actor may be forgiven in exchange for compelling dramatic performances. For example, despite the evident failure of his economic policies during his first two years in office, Ronald Reagan maintained a much higher level of popular support than less skilled presidential actors could have expected under similar circumstances. Many people seemed willing to grant Reagan large measures of sincerity and good intentions. How can people make such attributions about the offstage character of a public actor except by exercising implicit judgments about the quality of his onstage dramatic performances? Can such judgments really differ greatly from similar public attributions of sincerity and goodwill that made Reagan, earlier in his career, a successful television salesman for home appliances and soap powders?

In the world of political drama, the performance counts more than the success or failure of action, for, as noted in Chapter 2, the performance *is* the action as far as the public is concerned. Consider some cases of similar actions that were either made or broken by the quality of the surrounding dramatic performances. When John Kennedy admitted to botching the Bay of Pigs invasion, he was forgiven by a majority of Americans on the strength of his compassionate and convincing apology. Yet when Jimmy Carter took responsibility for the aborted attempt to rescue the American hostages from Iran, his popularity plunged. Carter, unlike Kennedy, had failed to script a dramatic performance that fit his role properly into the surrounding adventure saga. In short, Carter gave a bad performance. When Richard Nixon was a candidate for vice president in 1952, he faced the nation on television to address charges of political corruption. He won millions of voters' hearts with his careful script, his calculated stage setting, the fine supporting role of his faithful wife, and his emotionally delivered reference to his innocent little dog, Checkers. By contrast, when Nixon again faced corruption charges over two decades later, his performance was flawed, petulant, personal, and poorly rehearsed. He failed to produce the all-encompassing script and well-rehearsed supporting cast that represented his only conceivable salvation from the otherwise tawdry reality of the Watergate affair.

If the dramatization of political reality is a key to understanding the fortunes of public life, it is no less important for understanding the private political worlds of individual citizens. Vicarious political experience may be different from direct participation, but it is nonetheless a form of experience. Escape and entertainment are far from being meaningless pursuits. Whatever their other effects may be, political dramas can help people open up their fantasies and subconscious feelings with the result of relieving psychological tensions and easing social strains. The escape and entertainment functions of the news thus pave the way for important social and psychological adjustments.

Social and Psychological Adjustment

When people escape into the world of drama found in the news, they do not necessarily leave all their concerns behind them. Although our inclinations for direct action may be inhibited by the one-way communication channels of the mass media, we respond psychologically to the people and issues in news reports. It is, in fact, remarkably easy to identify with or against actors in the news, respond to them emotionally, and imagine that we are somehow part of their experiences. This sort of response to the news is possible because we have the capacity to generate fantasies.

Human beings spend a good deal of their waking and sleeping time creating imaginary scenarios in which they explore wishes, hopes, fears, and desires. Through fantasies we can rehearse unfamiliar social roles and anticipate encounters with other people. Fantasies also enable us to contain powerful feelings like anger, sexual desire, or fear when they are inappropriate to express openly in a particular situation. In other situations, fantasies help in making choices about how best to express those feelings in public.

A healthy fantasy life is essential for adjusting to the conditions and people we encounter in real life. The news, with its powerful images, emotional themes, and colorful characters, is a rich source of fantasy material. It is possible to step into a news plot and imagine what it would be like to be rich, poor, powerful, weak, female, male, sexy, brave, or intelligent. By taking the real world into the privacy of our minds via the news, we can explore feelings in ways that might not be comfortable in real life. We can relate to people in ways that would not be possible in real life.

Fantasies require very little anchor in reality in order to thrive. In fact, since fantasies involve, by definition, the suspending of ordinary reality, they can spring from the barest of suggestions and the least substantial of images. As far as our fantasy life goes, what does it matter what our favorite newscaster is really like in private life? As long as he or she displays the right style, manner, or looks, we feel comfortable inviting him or her into our home and listening as we would to a trusted friend imparting all the "news" that has transpired since we last got together. CBS anchorperson Dan Rather probably changed very little as a result of adding a sweater vest to soften his video image, but that small change of image apparently helped many viewers incorporate him into their fantasy lives.

Since fantasies feed from such minimal information, and since the news transmits such condensed, ambiguous images, it should not be surprising to learn that different people can generate very different fantasies from the same story. Who knows what it is really like to be the guerrilla fighter dashing through the jungle, locked in a life-or-death strugggle for the freedom of her country? Some might imagine that she is a romantic figure, with virtues like bravery, charisma, morals, and intelligence—the sort of person they would secretly like to be. Others might imagine her as a bloodthirsty heathen—an immoral communist who threatens their values and life styles. Same news story, different fantasies.

Part of the fantasy element in the news is caused by the heavy emphasis in politics on fantasy themes having to do with power, community, order, and security. Such concerns are central to the social and emotional well-being of the average person. Find a political speech without an emphasis on power, community, order, or security, and you have found an atypical and in all likelihood ineffectual political statement. These "fantasy themes"[7] of politics would never make it to the mass audience if the news did not transmit them.

It is hardly surprising that the news transmits fantasy themes from political performances to political audiences. In fact, mass media journalism tends to focus on fantasy themes. These themes, after all, represent the most dramatic and universally appealing components of political performances. Moreover, fantasy themes are about the only medium through which a lengthy political performance can be condensed into a meaningful news-length capsule.

In many cases, the news even boosts the emphasis on powerful images and fantasy themes over what it may have been in an actual political performance. Various techniques of storytelling, scene setting, and audio and visual display can be used to upgrade the fantasy level of an event. Consider, as an example, television news coverage of the Reagan inaugural. High rituals of state like inaugurations, campaigns, funerals, state of the union addresses, and the like offer a good vantage for viewing fantasy themes in action. These rituals are designed to appeal to the popular imagination with images of strength, community, security and new beginnings. Inaugurals are always occasions for calling the people together, reminding them that they are one nation with common bonds, and calling for renewal commitment to the goals of prosperity, harmony, peace, and security.

Since most people are preoccupied at some level with concerns about prosperity, harmony, peace, and security, it is comforting to have related fantasies evoked time and again by each new leader chosen to preserve and protect these elements of the American fantasy, more commonly referred to as the "American dream." Inaugural speeches are open invitations for new Presidents to pull out all the symbolic stops in an effort to kindle the deepest fantasies that define the political community.

Ronald Reagan was faced with a challenge when he mounted the platform to address the nation in 1980. The country was plunging into recession, national pride was at an ebb, and people saw a future with little promise. Drawing on the themes that got him elected, Reagan exhorted the country to step back into the past as a means of finding the values and spirit with which to face the future. He chose the perfect setting for such a speech. Standing at the West Front of the Capitol, Reagan could point to the great gallery of monuments that fill the national shrine of Washington, D.C. As he mentioned great heroes and episodes from the nation's past, he could evoke their physical presence at the same time. Mentioning George Washington is one thing, but filling the mind with the dramatic image of the Washington Monument and its stunning reflecting pool is an even more effective means of engaging the imagination of the audience.

In order to realize the full potential of the images in his speech, Reagan needed a little help from the media. He could, of course, talk about the great monuments and symbols of state that surrounded him, but how much more effective it would be if the media incorporated pictures of those things as though they were part of the script for the performance. Somehow Reagan and his media advisers must have anticipated what the journalists would do. All the White House needed to do was announce the time and place of the performance, issue an advance copy of the script, and the media could be relied on to do the rest. As the following excerpt from Ernest Bormann's analysis of inaugural coverage by CBS television indicates, journalist and political actor joined forces smoothly to maximize the fantasy potential in the event:

> Toward the close of the speech Reagan noted that this was the first time the ceremony was held on the West Front of the capitol, then he said, "Standing here, one faces a magnificent vista (The director called up a long shot of the magnificent vista), opening up on this city's special beauty and history. At the end of this open mall (The director had the camera pan up the open mall) are those shrines to the giants on whose shoulders we stand. Directly in front of me, the monument to a monumental man: (Cut to a shot of

Washington monument) George Washington, father of our country. ...."
After an encomium to Washington Reagan said, "Off to one side (Cut to a
shot of the Jefferson Memorial), the stately memorial to Thomas Jefferson."
After some words of praise for Jefferson, Reagan continued, "and then
beyond the reflecting pool, the dignified columns of the Lincoln Memorial
(Camera moves to Lincoln Memorial)." When Reagan next directed his audience's attention to the "sloping hills of Arlington National Cemetery with its
row upon row of simple white markers bearing crosses or Stars of David ...."
the director had the camera focus on the cemetery.[8]

With this kind of interplay between political images and news emphasis, it is little wonder that news represents a rich source of fantasy for
people. Indeed, the responses of participants in the News Research Project indicated a good deal of fantasy and emotional resonance with issues
and actors in the news. Two characteristics of such fantasy play are the
formation of strong expressions of feeling and opinion (stronger than
would ordinarily be acceptable in real life situations) and the development of vicarious relationships with the actors in news stories. Communication theorists have used the term "parasocial relationship" to refer
to the often intimate emotional bonds that people can establish with the
distant actors on the other end of one-way, mass media relationships.[9]
The responses of participants in the News Research Project indicated
that people had developed highly personalized relationships with actors
in the news, relationships that had blossomed safely over the vast dis-
tances of the mass communication wires. The level of emotional expression in many of the news evaluations was as intense as might be expected
in the most intimate of real social relationships. Also indicative of the
fantasy level on which parasocial relationships operate was the stream-of-
consciousness form of many responses. For example, an evaluation of a
presidential speech included the following statement about the speaker:
"President Reagan-Wealthy-Elitist-Bigot-Friend of the Rich-Foe of the
Poor and Handicapped-Poorly Read-Always the Mediocre Actor."
"Wealthy-Elitist-Bigot." Those strong terms are both emotionally ex-
pressive and representative of social bonds and antagonisms that have
been established with the outer world. Such reactions to people and issues
in political reporting can be important for purposes of emotional adjustment and maintaining a sense of emotional belonging in a vast and
alienating society. Whereas people often feel pressure not to express their
true feelings in real-life settings, they can rail against injustice and political folly through private interactions with the media. Similarly, although it
may be hard for people to take the measure of their group memberships
in real life, a range of clear-cut, simplified, and easily accessible social ties
and antagonisms are displayed on a daily basis in the news. The social and

emotional adjustment functions served by media politics may be more satisfying than the corresponding outlets for emotional expression and social bonding in everyday life.

What Price Mass-Mediated Reality?

Convenient as it may be for people to invest emotions and social commitments in neatly packaged media dramas, some costs are part of the bargain. These costs are reflected in the quality of the social communities in which people live. If the mass audience increasingly invests feelings and social bonds in media relationships because they are less threatening than real relationships, the quality of social life is likely to decline. People may increasingly remove important values and beliefs from the foundations of relationships. While it may be true that relationships built on things people value and care about are risky and emotionally volatile, the alternative is empty and meaningless. Friendships and associations based on nothing more than life styles, sports, games, play, or convenience are liable to dissolve as quickly as they were formed. People in such relationships cannot count on one another for support or trust. In fact, the withholding of true feelings about politics and society can become grounds for mutual paranoia, alienation, and suspicion.

People in modern society often work at maintaining social distance and cultivating casual relationships. At the same time, if talk shows, bestseller lists, and the latest human development fads are any indicator, people seem preoccupied with how to restore meaning and feeling in their social lives. It would seem that people are in a bind. The convenience of fantasy relationships may be too tempting to resist, yet the poverty of real society is too painful to ignore.

Beyond the social consequences of a mass-mediated reality there lie some important political effects. If people find emotional and social significance in the distant world of news politics, the media and the government are in possession of a powerful mechanism of political and social control. The temptation always exists for political actors to propose magical solutions and fantastic political scenarios through the use of myths, stereotypes, scapegoats, and other symbolic devices. When the media legitimize such techniques and in the process condition the public to accept them, there are no restraints on the fabrication of political reality. Under such circumstances, political actors can manage issues, conflicts, and crises by simply throwing symbols at them—symbols that may be irrelevant to the matters at hand yet that provoke powerful emotional responses from the public. For example, during the public debate in Congress in 1982 over U.S. policy toward El Salvador, the State Department continued to make alarming statements that the civil war was promoted by outside communist intervention. Senators spoke of the need to help our "friends" in the Salvadoran government in their struggle for freedom. Such statements persisted even after no conclusive evidence of massive outside communist assistance was produced. The Secretary of State claimed that such evidence existed but could not be presented for national security reasons having to do with the protection of intelligence sources. The Salvadoran government continued to be called a "friend" in the struggle for freedom, even though it perpetrated the murder, rape, torture of upward of 10,000 innocent civilians each year (a rather large terrorism program for a small, freedom-loving country). The White House even issued repeated reports to the effect that there had been significant improvements in the human rights policies of that "democratic" government—reports that must have been regarded as empty symbolic statements by those who issued them and those who used them for propaganda purposes.

Nevertheless, what may be an empty symbolic statement to the authority who issued it can become filled quickly with feeling and meaning by a confused public looking for simple and satisfying solutions for political and social problems. Even though opponents in Congress were heard to attack the government propaganda campaign on El Salvador as a sham, the news audience was faced once again with its standard dilemma: the acceptance of unprovable accusations against the authorities who control information, and manufacture propaganda to suit their policies, versus the acceptance of the propaganda. The propaganda has the attractions of being officially endorsed, represented in the news as at least one legitimate alternative, and, above all, emotionally satisfying. It is so much simpler and easier to cast one's feeling on the side of democracy and throw one's social antagonisms against the communists than it is to work out a personal understanding of the situation, particularly when such an understanding will be rejected by the authorities elected to handle the problem and condemned by fellow citizens who find it easier to follow the course of least emotional resistance.

If these two trends toward the suppression of feelings in real life and the displacement of social and emotional ties on distant political symbols continue, the most unsettling effect of all may result. People may grow gradually to expect, and even depend on, the media to provide them with outlets for their social and emotional needs. If people find satisfaction in the fantasy scenarios of mass media politics (not to mention television programs, movies, commercials, etc.), it may cease to matter how far removed from reality those fantasy objects may be. The public may become conditioned to the emotional manipulation that oppresses them. George Orwell may have been a few years too hasty in making his terrifying predictions about 1984, but the seeds of what he was talking about already exist in the psychological bonds that join government, media, and the people in their current political union.

Notes

1. The *News Research Project* was the first phase of a larger study of political issue formation funded by the National Science Foundation under grant #SES80–25046, W. Lance Bennett, principal investigator.
2. For an introduction to the "uses and gratifications" concept, see Jay G. Blumler and Denis McQuail, *Television in Politics: Its Uses and Influences* (Chicago: University of Chicago Press, 1969). Also, Lee B. Becker, "Two Tests of Media Gratification: Watergate and the 1974 Elections," *Journalism Quarterly* 53 (1976): 26–31.
3. See, for example, Dan Berlyne, *Conflict, Arousal, and Curiosity* (New York: McGraw–Hill, 1960).
4. For an explanation of how such scripts are formed and how they work, see Roger Schank and Robert Abelson, *Scripts, Plans, Goals and Understanding* (Hillsdale, N.J.: Lawrence Erlbaum, 1977).
5. For a discussion of how new stimuli become incorporated into a mental picture, see W. Lance Bennett, "Perception and Cognition: An Information-Processing Framework for Politics," *The Handbook of Political Behavior, vol. 1*, ed. Samuel Long (New York: Plenum, 1981).
6. Walter Lippmann, *Public Opinion* (New York: Free Press, 1922).
7. "Fantasy Theme" is a concept coined by Ernest G. Bormann in his article "The Eagleton Affair: A Fantasy Theme Analysis," *Quarterly Journal of Speech* 59 (1973): 143–59.
8. From Ernest G. Bormann, "A Fantasy Theme Analysis of the Television Coverage of the Hostage Release and the Reagan Inaugural," *Quarterly Journal of Speech* 68 (1982): 137–38.
9. See, for example, Donald Horton and R. Richard Wohl, "Mass Communication and Para-Social Interaction," *Psychiatry* 19 (1956): 219–29; see also Mark R. Levy, "Watching TV News as Para Social Interaction," *Journal of Broadcasting* 23 (Winter 1979): 69–80.

FIVE

Freedom from the Press

News from the past
> Where the press is free, and every
> man able to read, all is safe.

THOMAS JEFFERSON

News in the future?
> The critics say it's a new art form—a
> mixture of news, documentary and
> drama serial .... Part of what
> excites people is that they never
> know if what they're watching is
> real action ... or if it's staged. You
> can think whatever turns you on the
> most .... [I]t's the last stage of the
> spectacle—a sort of living room
> bread-and-circuses with the copout
> of letting you pretend it's not real.

MARGE PIERCY

News is usually defined as *information that is timely, relevant to the con-cerns of its audience, and presented in a form that is easy to grasp.* If this definition is taken at face value, the news serves the noble purpose of providing a window on the world for the masses. However, it should be clear at this point that each component of the above definition operates in the real world with hidden defects which, when taken together, make mass media news anything but an adequate representation of the social world.

The News Is Timely . . .

In a sense most news is timely, with the biggest stories being those late-breaking events that are often in progress at the time the news is re-ported. The hidden defect of timeliness entails a loss of perspective on events, however. To begin with, the reporter rushing out to cover a breaking story often has little frame of reference about the event other

125

than what can be imported into the situation via standardized reporting formulas. In the words of one observer: "A reporter can seldom know as he sets out to cover an event whether it will be banal or significant."[1] Thus, events are often frozen arbitrarily for purposes of casting them as news. Journalistic formulas give such suspended events their meanings, while the element of timeliness provides a semblance of exaggerated yet fleeting importance. At the same time that the timeliness of news exaggerates the importance of rapidly unfolding events, it diminishes the visibility of situations that are less episodic in nature. Important human problems like poverty, alienation, powerlessness, and diminishing life quality seldom appear in the headlines.

In addition to promoting formula reporting and distorting the importance of events, timeliness contributes to news fragmentation. Old events are shuttled out of the headlines as soon as new ones are available to take their place. Timeliness permits little consideration of how important the replacement stories are, or what happened to the ones that they replaced. Follow-up stories are few in number and seldom receive prominent coverage. Timely news presents a world in dramatic change, but it is a world in which events are disconnected and change has little direction.

The News Is Relevant . . .

The hidden effects of timeliness also spill over into the second defining characteristic of news: relevance. As noted above, events that unfold rapidly and dramatically are made to seem relevant because they are urgently reported; permanent but unchanging conditions become invisible and, for all practical purposes, irrelevant. Thus, the decades of grinding poverty, exploitation, and oppression suffered by the people in El Salvador were scarcely reported by the American news media. Then, suddenly, there was guerrilla warfare, and the drama of revolution made the news. Why, the American people must have wondered, was there such a sudden explosion in El Salvador? Officials in San Salvador and Washington pronounced the trouble the result of communist infiltration from Nicaragua, Cuba, and Russia—nations bent on importing revolution into peaceful, democratic countries. The credibility of such an absurd explanation depended in large part on the virtual absence of prior coverage of the decades of poverty, misery, and government terrorism that led to the popular uprising.

As noted, when the conditions that precede an event go unreported, they become irrelevant to the news audience. Yet that same audience requires some context in which to place the events in the news. At the same time, journalists who are caught unawares by the latest-breaking crisis search for some instant framework that will condense months and years of missing history into the capsule of the present moment. Both the public and the press fall easy prey to government officials who write the scripts for rapidly unfolding news stories.

And so, an ending was written for the El Salvador story. The "communist plot" justified a massive infusion of U.S. military aid. The national army was strengthened, and the people's army grew weak. An election was staged to show that democracy flourished in the country. The vote was proclaimed a victory for democracy and a defeat for communism. The government, armed with its symbolic mandate and new weapons, launched a major offensive against the guerrillas. The country was declared stable once again. At last the eye of the news could turn away from El Salvador, leaving behind the same poverty, oppression, corruption, and exploitation that existed before. Should the depleted citizenry fight the odds and oppose the government once again, the news would return. And it would bring along with it the same distorted sense of relevance that it brought before.

Timeliness is just one factor that affects considerations of relevance in the news. As the El Salvador story indicates, journalists also employ a number of substantive criteria in deciding what is relevant to report. It is clear, for example, that information becomes more relevant when it is offered to the press by "credible" news sources for public consumption. Since reporters cannot presume to know what is in the interest of the public, they allow authorities to make such judgments implicitly. Moreover, when a story begins to build toward some predictable conclusion, officials who can vouch for that conclusion gain ever greater control over the information that enters the news. For example, when elections were staged and dramatized as a "test of democracy" in El Salvador, the news later became dominated by officials who proclaimed the election results to be a decisive victory for freedom. Thus the political ending of the story was written before there was a chance to see how well it squared with reality. It was several weeks until it became clear that the elections had restored power to the most authoritarian elements in the country. It was fully a month or more before indicators of massive vote fraud began to surface. Unfortunately, the conclusion to the news story had already been written by the time these elements of reality began to intrude.

A second substantive component of news relevance involves reporters' decisions about what the audience is capable of grasping about an event. No matter how much a news story is dominated by official propaganda, reporters must still exercise discretion about what background information to include, what official perspectives to emphasize, and how to pitch the story to the audience. Although it would be nice to think that reporters could use the news to educate the public about developing situations, the norm of objectivity forces reporters to let actors and events do as much of the talking as possible. It is hard to find instant events that illustrate decades of history that the news has lost. The task of explaining current events becomes awesome. Journalists who face this task find it convenient to assume that the public is capable of grasping only the simplest messages and images. Thus, struggles for independence in the Third World can be reduced to convenient formulas about the struggle between democracy and communism—such formulas import their own historical assumptions, however irrelevant they may be, into the vacant news frame. Similarly, American elections are reduced to "horseraces." Economic trends become cartoonlike struggles between wages and prices, spending and saving, labor and management.

A third element of news relevance is the effort to incorporate the "other side" of the story into the news frame whenever possible. Although it seems reasonable to suppose that information is more relevant (i.e., useful and objective) when it is balanced, it is worth considering whether the sort of balance achieved in most news stories amounts to much. In many cases the basic plot of the news story has already been written by the time the "other side" is incorporated. When story angles are initiated through prepared official statements and further narrowed through journalistic formulas, the information provided by the "other side" becomes a foregone conclusion. As a result, guerrillas in El Salvador become communists or socialists no matter what their political message may be. Workers in most labor disputes are seen as pressing for higher wages no matter what other issues are involved. Candidates in an election are saddled with their positions in the horserace no matter what substantive considerations may govern their candidacies. Can you imagine how different elections would be if the media were prohibited from announcing the standings of the candidates in the opinion polls prior to the election?

Even when official views and formula plots do not render the other side of a story irrelevant, many other factors can damage the relevance of "two sided" information. It may even be the case that forcing people to consider both sides of every issue is more numbing than clarifying in its overall effects. For example, disclosures about public health hazards related to food, consumer products, auto safety, or industrial pollution are often reported along with counterclaims of corporate representatives or government officials. It is not clear that such "boiler plate" denials are relevant to public understanding of a situation—in all likelihood, they make it difficult for people to know what to think. Thus the element of confusion takes its place alongside propaganda and stereotype in the working definition of news relevance.

The News Is Easy to Grasp . . .

The final defining property of news is that it conveys information in a manner that is easy for people to grasp. In practical terms this means that mass media news is almost always packaged in the form of stories. Most of those stories are formula stories. Although few journalists would agree that they trade in formula news, most would acknowledge that the story is the basic communication format of the profession. The use of stories has been defended over the past hundred years as the most efficient and broadly understood means of transmitting social information. Stories are, after all, the things people use to exchange information about their everyday lives. As such, stories are broadly used and easy to interpret.

While there is little doubt that stories are easy to grasp, it is less clear what people actually grasp from them. Even in everyday life, stories permit people enormous room for reconstructing reality. It is true, of course, that all forms of communication operate on reality in one way or another—that is the whole point of communication. Nevertheless, stories differ in significant ways from other forms of information transmission such as theories, logical arguments, ideological analyses, or scientific methods. Consider just two features that make stories the least disciplined of all information structures.

First, stories pick up facts from the real world and put very narrow and selective boundaries around them. For example, since stories are best equipped to describe the acts of individuals, group behaviors in the news are often reduced to the exploits of single leaders or the experiences of a few rank-and-file members. As a result, stories make it difficult to think about groups as anything other than collections of single actors. If stories reduce groups to their individual members, they are even less capable of presenting a clear picture of social forces. The news is hard pressed to explain structural conditions in society (e.g., the bases of political power or the workings of credit and banking) except as these conditions involve individual actors. We may hear how the President used his influence to get the Federal Reserve Bank to lower the discount rate. Such a story cannot touch on most of the important questions about government and banking: Do Presidents have any long-term control over the Federal Reserve? Does a temporary change in Federal Reserve policy serve any purpose other than to help struggling Presidents at election time? Who really runs the Federal Reserve? What is the Federal Reserve anyhow?

By reducing events to the simplistic exploits of the heroes and villains who occupy center stage, stories make it hard to think clearly about the outer world. Fact becomes lost in fantasy. Cause and effect are reduced to microscopic terms. Yet the parade of new heroes and villains (and the old ones doing new things) creates the illusion of a world in change and motion. The encapsulation of all this action within the narrow boundaries of a story allows the audience to ignore the lack of broader substance behind the illusion. Packaging the news in stories helps assure the accuracy of the adage that "the more things change, the more they stay the same."

A second property of stories that is worth noting is that they are very subjective interpretations of events. Stories are bound less by the demands of reality than by the storyteller's decisions about how to reconstruct reality. The entire point of a story can change depending on how the scene is set, which characters are included, what actions are emphasized, and how the circumstances surrounding the actions are presented.[2] It is no exaggeration to say that any event lends itself to multiple stories and that each story changes the meaning of the event (try it). Even though we may be accustomed to hearing mythical editors instruct their reporters to "get me *the* story," it is important to recognize that there is no such thing as *the* story. For example, instead of arranging a set of facts about El Salvador into a story of the struggle between freedom and communism, the media could have organized the facts differently to tell the dramatic story of the valiant struggle of a people to win freedom from their own government—a struggle defeated largely through the efforts of the United States. Yet a story like the latter one could not have been told without disrupting the delicate illusion of objectivity. Such a story would have pitted the media squarely against its main source of objectivity—the government. Such a story would have shown how fragile facts become when spun into stories.

It is amazing that a medium as inherently subjective as the story has acquired a veneer of objectivity through its use by journalists. As noted in Chapter 3, this semblance of objectivity has been acquired largely through the implicit standardization of news plots—a standardization that is possible only through the implicit cooperation of political actors and journalists. The standardization of reality is, of course, a convincing substitute for objectivity. As Paletz and Entman have observed, the plots of news stories have become so routine that "they are not perceived by journalists or politicians or the public as interpretive frames at all, but as objective facts."[3] Robert Scholes developed this idea a bit further when he said: "Perhaps the credulous believe that a reporter reports facts and that newspapers print all of them that are fit to print. But actually, newspapers print all of the 'facts' that fit, period—that fit the journalistic conventions of what 'a story' is (those tired formulas) and that fit the editorial policy of the paper. . . ."[5] Anyone for changing that famous slogan to "All the News that Fits, We Print"?

As the above problems indicate, the use of stories as the means of making the news "graspable" has the most sweeping effects of all the defining characteristics of the news. The requirement for drama in a good story invites the use of staged political performances. The subjectivity of storytelling promotes a faked objectivity that depends on standardized political scripts coauthored by politicians and reporters. Finally, the narrow, personalized, dramatic qualities of stories invite the public to indulge fantasies rather than engage critical thinking when it comes to the news. In short, the use of stories combines with the practical aspects of timeliness and relevance to subordinate the facts in the news to the political messages promoted by a select few newsmakers and journalists. That sort of news is no mirror on the world. Rather, the news becomes a distorting lens through which selected aspects of the world are brought into focus, while the rest of the picture is reduced to a permanent blur.

Why the News Illusion Persists: News, Power, and Belief

The majority of citizens, politicians, and journalists seem blind to the way in which the whole set of political and journalistic activities involved with "objective" reporting have subverted the ideals of timely, relevant, interpretable news. In fact, when the failings of the news are discussed, they are most often blamed on the failure of the press to be objective enough! It seems that people have thoroughly mistaken the cause of the problem for its solution.

Think for a moment about what it means to say that the news should be more "objective." The demand for greater objectivity is usually based on the charge that reporters introduce their own personal, usually "liberal," bias into their reporting. Thus the call for more objective or neutral news really means that reporters should report only what newsmakers (who are most often government officials) want to have reported. It follows, therefore, that the more neutral, middle-of-the-road, or "objective" the news becomes, the more it also becomes a pure advertisement for established authority. Objectivity and political authority thus become one and the same. Truly "objective" information, in this warped sense of the term, would be narrow, intolerant of diverse political values, and uncritical of authority. It is rather ironic to think that the most important prescription for restoring the ideals of timely, relevant interpretable news would, if carried out, completely subvert those ideals.

In order to think more realistically about news reform, we must first understand the true cause of the problem and then understand why most people are unable to accept it, or even to see it clearly. Up to this point in the book, the cause of news distortion has been explained in terms of the whole set of political and journalistic activities involved with objective reporting. These activities are, indeed, the immediate causes of problems with the news, but what explains the dogged persistence of these journalistic and political practices? The whole set of political and journalistic activities that have subverted the news can be traced to a rather disturbing root cause: the place of news in the American power structure. As we shall see, politicians, journalists, and the public are locked into a set of power relations that reinforces political deception, promotes journalistic narrowness and deference to authority, and encourages public ignorance and retreat into a political fantasy world.

Why is it so hard for people to see that the news is a distorted reflection of the power structure in which the people have increasingly less power while the political and economic elite have ever more power? Here we enter the world of belief and opinion. There exists in American society a powerful climate of opinion that promotes the idea of a free press and a free people. This climate of opinion is sufficiently strong that doubters are likely to suppress (or at least not express) their concerns about information control and loss of power, while the majority of "true believers" are likely to be uncritical in their beliefs about freedom of information and democracy in America.

In short, the problem of news reform is a profound one that involves the realities of political power and the illusions of political belief. The realities of power have created the problem, while the illusions of belief make it impossible for most people to even see the problem clearly, much less think about realistic solutions for it. Clarifying these relations among power, belief, and news is a first step toward a realistic response to the news problem.

News and Power in America

In the ideal civics book version of American democracy, power rests with the people. The people, in effect, are the voice of the political system. Leaders are supposed to take cues from the people and express their voice politically. The journalist in this scheme occupies the role of the independent "monitor" who reports to the people on how well leaders handle the public trust. In simple picture form, this ideal version of power in America looks like Figure 1.

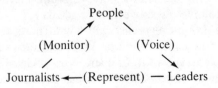

FIGURE 1

It is obvious that the reality of power in America does not look much like this ideal picture. As numerous examples in the book have indicated, leaders have usurped enormous amounts of political power and reduced popular control over the political system by using the media to generate support, compliance, and just plain confusion among the public. People may be given some range of choice by the ruling elite, but the substance of that choice is determined more by politicians and media than by people. The media also occupy a different role in the reality of American politics than the one they are supposed to play in the ideal version. Far from being monitors of the elite, the media have become political transmission lines to the people. The media not only send political messages to the public but also screen the reactions of people to those messages. Thus, even when people attempt to respond to their leaders, those responses are translated into standard reporting formulas that redefine public reactions, underplay fundamental dissatisfactions, exaggerate short-term frustrations, and move issues out of the range of public attention as rapidly as possible. The media thus reinforce the legitimacy of power from above while defusing the demands for power from below. The roles of elites and the media in this power structure clearly relegate the power of the people to the bottom of the heap. The public is exposed to powerful persuasive messages from above, and is unable to communicate meaningfully through the media in response to those messages. A more realistic picture of American political power looks something like Figure 2.

FIGURE 2

Where is the impetus for change in the news likely to come from in this scheme of things? Surely not from below. If the news distorts communication both going to and coming from the people, it is hard to imagine how the public could organize an effective movement to change the nature of politics and information in America. To begin with, it is hard for people to conceive of political actions that fly in the face of the pronouncements of the highest authorities in the land, pronouncements that are given the stamp of authenticity by an independent press. And even when people become frustrated enough to demand more realistic and useful political information, they find it difficult to form effective political movements because the lines of communication are controlled by those who are most threatened by such a change. It is hard to take meaningful action when the meaning of one's acts is scripted by the opposition.

If an information reform movement is unlikely to come from below, it is virtually inconceivable that it will emerge from the top of the power structure. To ask politicians to disclose their true thoughts, goals, and actions would be to ask them to give up the thing they most value and need: power. Only those leaders who wish to give up power will give up information. Such leaders do not last long at the top.

Power and information have become so intertwined at the top levels of government that it is no longer clear that reporters would find much meaningful information even if they could investigate behind the scenes of government activities. With the rare exception of cases like the Watergate tapes, it is fanciful to suppose that something called "the truth" exists in the filing cabinets behind the locked doors of government offices. Successful political actors have learned that it is best to manufacture the truth to fit their political goals.

Yet it is still comforting to think we live in a simple world where the truth exists if only politicians will tell it to us. It is reassuring to think that we still live in the nineteenth-century world of politics and information described in John Hohenberg's anecdote about a confrontation between General Sherman and an enterprising reporter. Sherman threw the reporter out of his office after the reporter had demanded information about Sherman's activities. The reporter protested that he was only seeking the truth. Sherman replied: "That's what we don't want! We don't want the truth told about things here."[5]

In the modern world of politics, power depends so much on the complete control of information that information is often manufactured to suit the political designs of its users. The hierarchy of power becomes unshakable when leaders do not have to worry about hiding the truth because they have gained control over the bureaucracies and intelligence organizations that manufacture the information on which the truth rests. Consider an example of what this sort of information control does to the prospects for more insightful political reporting.

Both during and after the Vietnam war, it had been rumored that the U.S. Army had falsified its estimates of enemy troop strength and enemy battle deaths. The underestimation of enemy troop strength and the overestimation of body counts would have been useful ways of boosting the morale of the American public, who grew ever more weary of the endless war. Reports of higher death rates among fewer enemy troops gave cause for optimism and shored up public support for government war policies.

It wasn't until fourteen years after the first rumors of Intelligence falsification began to appear that a CBS news documentary gave them legitimate news coverage. In a 1982 exposé titled "The Uncounted Enemy—A Vietnam Deception," former intelligence personnel reported that they encountered pressures to manufacture unrealistic figures on enemy strength. The documentary was immediately attacked by both the government and former Army Commander William Westmoreland, who was accused of directing the Intelligence falsification. Westmoreland brought a multimillion-dollar slander suit against CBS.

Let's interrupt the story at this stage to draw two points out of it. First, we have here a classic case of government power (in this case, the power to wage a war) depending on information control that worked long after the policy of the government had ended. The American people can hardly be expected to participate in their government when they are kept in the dark both during and after the events that affect their lives have unfolded. Second, even this rare, after-the-fact news report on information control elicited a massive political and legal reprisal from the parties involved. It is, to say the least, costly for news organizations to reveal the true workings of power and information in American politics.

But our story is not over. There is still the matter of whether, in the final analysis, the charges of falsification of figures can ever be made to stick. If, in the end, the issue boils down to a few former low-level officials saying that facts were falsified, and a few high-level officials saying that the figures were simply the best available estimates—who is to say who is right? Former State Department official Hodding Carter III provided a key insight into this problem of information verification when he noted that by the end of the war, all the government intelligence agencies were coming up with virtually identical estimates of enemy troop strength. Carter noted in a *Wall Street Journal* editorial that in the early years of the war, the Central Intelligence Agency had disagreed with Army Intelligence estimates. The CIA even argued its case with the President, but quickly realized that the point of intelligence wasn't always to produce accurate information. As Carter (and CBS) noted: "The CIA's analysts repeatedly challenged the [army] figures during much of 1967, but when a showdown on the figures arose, the CIA's top brass apparently decided that sticking with the truth made for bad bureaucratic politics, since it put the agency at odds with the President, and they backed away temporarily. The military analysts who knew better decided to play good soldier. The American people knew nothing of this and instead were fed a stream of statements claiming that the enemy's ranks were being steadily depleted."[6]

The problem hidden in this scenario is that when intelligence-gathering procedures begin to fit information to the needs of government policy, there is no longer any hard information with which to prove the case against the government. In fact, just the opposite is true: All the "best" information produced by the "best" intelligence methods is perfectly in line with what the government told the people. The most thorough investigative reporting can do no more than pit one person's word against another. Such high-level shouting matches are seldom satisfying, for they cannot fully resolve the doubts of an "objectivity-minded" public who suspend their judgments about truth until they see hard, undisputed facts. The days of independent and conclusive facts are rapidly coming to an end in the modern information state. Yet the ideal of objectivity lingers on.

Consider another example that foretells the "end of objectivity." In his discussion of the CBS Vietnam documentary, Hodding Carter went on to draw a parallel with more recent government actions in El Salvador. One of the conditions attached to U.S. grants of military and economic aid to El Salvador was that the Salvadoran government had to distribute farmland to thousands of hungry, powerless, and exploited citizens. The U.S. government estimated that there were some 125,000 families eligible to receive farmland. Following two years of "rumors" that the land-reform program was a sham, the U.S. State Department released a report concluding that the program was working smoothly. The report concluded that nearly one third of all eligible families had received land. The only problem was that the alleged success of the program was based on a government revision of its estimates of eligible families from 125,000 to 67,000. When questioned about the revision, the State Department (speaking through Deane Hinton, the ambassador to El Salvador) said simply that the new figure reflected "subsequent analysis based on the best available data."[7] To which Carter mused in his editorial: "Perhaps, and perhaps not. It may be only coincidental that the new arithmetic makes our policy position in El Salvador, and our client government there, look good. . . . Whence come the new figures? Not from U.S. officials, because the Agency for International Development has discontinued field checks on the land reform program because of dangerous conditions in the countryside."[8]

The most telling statement in Carter's commentary on the El Salvador land-reform question is one that can be applied equally well to dozens of government policy areas: "Does that mean this is another case of making the facts fit the policy? We have no way of knowing based on the available evidence. But if a scam is being pulled on us in the name of national policy once again, it would be nice if we didn't have to wait 14 years before those who know better come forward and blow the whistle. Great television exposés after the fact help us understand history, but in the meantime we're stuck with lousy policy."[9] Carter might have added that even if we find out about such information scams 14 years too late, we almost never have enough hard evidence to convincingly prove the case anyway—even if people cared that much about the facts of ancient history.

At some point, it must be recognized that the use of information to control political reality is an everyday occurrence. Information is the basis of power, and as a result, any change away from "objective" news reporting will be resisted by leaders who understand the subtle points of the information game. As Thomas Powers noted in a discussion of how intelligence agencies have fueled the international arms race:

> Dishonesty in the intelligence business is not personal but institutional. In effect, the analysts are advocates. The Air Force wants to build planes and missiles; the Navy wants to build ships; the Army wants more tanks and fully equipped divisions. All tend to think that the Russians see things the same way, and all "interpret" the evidence according to their own lights. The scantier the evidence—and it is always scanty at the beginning—the wilder the extrapolations. Since no one knows what the evidence means for sure, every National Intelligence Estimate is subject to negotiation, an intensely political process reflecting the realities of life in Washington.[10]

If changes in the nature of the information game are unlikely to come from the top or the bottom of the information-power structure, what about the middle? Are journalists truly trapped in a set of power relations that makes it impossible for them to see the contradictions in their commitment to "objectivity" and adopt a more realistic reporting strategy (such as ideological critique, theoretical analysis, or simple, logical political interpretation)? In some ways it would seem that journalists have the greatest margin of flexibility within the power structure. After all, this is still a liberal political system. The state does not own and operate the press. Freedom of speech is still protected by the courts. Dissident journalists are unlikely to be shot, tortured, or to simply "disappear." In most respects the elite could not operate in its current fashion without the tacit cooperation of the press. So, why will the media not take the monitor role seriously and provide information to the people in ways that might liberate them from the political communication trap discussed earlier?

There are, of course, a number of obvious reasons why the media do not monitor government actions in an adequate way. To begin with, the news as it currently exists is a successful, profit-making enterprise; news organizations have little incentive to change what they do. Moreover, journalists derive a large measure of professional success and personal life satisfaction from their jobs. Where is the incentive to rock the boat? It also must be noted that critical reporting often brings both subtle and overt forms of political pressure to bear on reporters and their organizations. As noted, for example, the political and legal responses to the CBS Vietnam report were imposing.

Even routine news reporting is constantly criticized by members of the political and economic elite for not being sufficiently "objective." Powerful people who are as secure and influential as Walter Wriston, the chairman of Citibank, act as if the best defense of their power is a good offense against the media:

> The media, supported by some academic "liberals," would have us believe that things are not just going badly, they are growing progressively and rapidly worse. The dominant theme is the new American way of failure. No one wins; we always lose. Jack Armstrong and Tom Swift are dead. If an individual says anything important, it is either ignored or nitpicked to death by commentators. . . . Let one scientist resign and say that nuclear power is a lethal accident waiting to happen, and he is awarded front page with pictures. He has unlimited interviews on television. The massive achievements of hundreds and hundreds of scientists and the comfort of millions of citizens who enjoy the products of nuclear power go for nothing. We daily see illustrated a point made by the jurist Oliver Wendell Holmes: "When the ignorant are taught to doubt, they do not know what they safely may believe." The media should beware of sowing the dragon's teeth of confusion.[11]

The world must look like a pretty rosy place from atop the Citicorp Tower. From that vantage, it must be frustrating to think that the public has the capacity to doubt. However, it is not clear that the rich and powerful see (or even live in) the same world that the rest of us live in. Yet the members of the corporate and political ranks spend a good deal of time convincing the public that we all share the same interests and that it is the press who have led us astray through doubt and confusion. When the authorities accuse the press of being nonobjective, they put journalists in the bind discussed in Chapter 3—the bind created by exposing the fragile nature of "objectivity." Even though these same authorities may be the ones guilty of sowing the seeds of doubt and confusion, the media must cave in ultimately if they wish to maintain the illusion of an objective world.

The chilling effects of profits, professionalism, and politics on journalistic incentives for news reform cannot be measured. Nevertheless, it would violate everything we know about newsgathering to suppose that those effects are not large. As if these obstacles to journalistic change were not enough, there are still others.

Profits and political pressures of the sort discussed thus far operate primarily at the highest levels of news organizations—in the boardrooms and executive offices where decisions are made about who to hire, who to fire, how much money to spend, and where to place the emphasis of news coverage. What about life in the trenches? Why does not the average reporter "blow the whistle" on the news game? Why are there not more critics among the rank-and-file press corps? Aside from social status, and the material comforts of the reporter's life, there are also aspects of the power structure that isolate and trap the individual journalist into upholding the illusion of objectivity.

In order to see how journalists operate within the power system it is, first, necessary to remember that the existence of a "free press" places journalists in competition with one another. They compete for exclusive interviews, for chances to ask questions at press conferences, for the privilege of early filing on big stories, and for friendly recognition from newsmakers. Even the most high-minded journalists are locked into this game of competition, and the resources they are competing for are controlled from above. People who compete for resources beyond their individual control often face a difficult situation known among game theorists as the "prisoner's dilemma." In a prisoner's dilemma situation, all players know that they share a common value and that it is in their interest to remain loyal to that value. Outside forces may enter the field of play and provide huge rewards to individuals who reject the common value position while heaping huge losses on players who maintain a commitment to the common good. If all the individuals reject the common good, however, their alternative reward is diminished because they all must share it. As a result, the individuals who leave the group position lose both the reward for defection and the group value left behind.

The reasons why people faced with a prisoner's dilemma often sacrifice the common good (only to suffer an even greater value loss) are illustrated with the example that gave the game its name. In criminal prosecutions, silence among thieves would foil many an attempt to gather enough evidence to convict any of them. In virtually all these situations, "honor among thieves" would promote the best interests of each and all. The prosecution is often in a position to destroy such honor by creating conditions of isolation and mutual suspicion among the individuals involved. Secret promises of little or no punishment made to one individual often produce defections in the form of "turning state's evidence" against those who choose not to cooperate. If all parties defect, however, then there is no lack of evidence and the case against all is strengthened. All the defectors end up losing. In view of the political structure of the game, the lack of honor among thieves has less to do with the character of the average criminal than with the circumstances under which he or she is brought to justice.

The commodity at stake in the news game is information or, more properly, its value as measured by how closely it matches the reality of a political situation. Reporters know that it is in the moral interest of each and all to uphold common commitments: to tell the truth, to resist the reporting of political deception, and to expose such deception whenever they know it to be present. Despite the clarity of the common interest, reporters often behave as though they were prisoners of their news sources, defecting from their positions of conscience instead of finding ways as a group to preserve their highest individual values. In any contrived newsmaking situation in which information is controlled effectively by a news source, the first reporter to "defect" from his or her position of conscience or group interest will be rewarded in any of a number of ways: with a scoop, or at least an early filing of the story; with preferential access to news sources, thereby assuring future scoops and future early filings; with a story that is easy to report because of the "self-documenting" property of pseudoevents; with a story that is easy to justify to an editor due to its clean, formulaic documentation, and so on. By contrast, reporters who adhere to a position of conscience will be punished disproportionately through loss of stories, access, editorial support, and perhaps even their jobs. As a result, reporters probably make regular individual decisions, no matter how distasteful, to defect from their true values and report news of dubious informational value. In short, the structure of the news game leads reporters to routinely generate winning strategies that are bound to lose.

As indicated by this brief overview, the players in the news game are locked into stable relationships that subvert the quality of information and the meaning of politics in America. And yet few people seem to see the situation as subversive—or at least few people are willing to acknowledge the situation as subversive. In fact, politicians, journalists, and the public tend to join ranks in proclaiming the freedom of the press and the importance of objective information. Therefore, if we are to understand American news politics, we must answer the question of why the ideal of objective news, with all its flaws, is so strongly defended by leaders, journalists, and citizens alike.

Believing in the News

Somewhere in the back of the mind of almost every citizen is a collection of inspiring images of the press. These images are based on the dramatic events and the guiding sentiments of American history, sentiments like the ones expressed in these words of Thomas Jefferson: "The people are the only censors of their governors [and they must have full] information of their affairs through the channel of the public papers . . . [Were] it left to me to decide whether we should have a government without newspapers or newspapers without a government, I should not hesitate a moment to prefer the latter."[12]

Ideas like these have been echoed by every generation of journalists, educators, and politicians throughout American history. When such guiding principles are passed down from generation to generation, they come to represent the spirit of a nation and a people. It ceases to matter much what those sentiments really mean, or whether they are even true. Ideas given such powerful reinforcement and endowing people with such noble purpose take on a life of their own. They are inspirational, hopeful, and ennobling. They give a sense of substance to a national history that would otherwise become vague in the minds of new generations. Such are the characteristics of myths.

Myths require little empirical proof to sustain them. They are taught to the children of society long before they are old enough to think or reason critically. They are reinforced throughout life with the words and acts of the most respected people in society. They are uttered by one and all as much out of a sense of abiding duty and social solidarity as out of any conviction based on evidence of their validity. In some cases, the powerful climate of opinion established by the universal proclamation of a myth is enough to force people to utter the words of a myth even when they may not believe them in private. It is likely, for example, that many citizens of Nazi Germany had little private commitment to the myth of Aryan superiority, and yet the powerful climate of opinion in the country induced virtually everyone to act as if they believed the superiority myth. When the majority acts as if they believe in something, it matters little what their private thoughts may be. The private doubts of millions of Germans did nothing to prevent the holocaust of World War II.

The point here is not to suggest that our most profound social beliefs rest entirely on a foundation of psychological conditioning, celebrity endorsement, and social pressure. Nevertheless, it would be a mistake to underestimate the importance of conditioning, authority, and social pressure in the construction of our social and political worlds. Beyond these social and psychological forces, myths also depend on some sort of functional payoff to keep them alive for long periods of time. Without some tangible benefits, the "free press, free people" myth (with its related beliefs about objective information) could not have endured as long as it has in American politics.

Just because myths usually serve some purpose for people, it does not necessarily follow that the beliefs surrounding the myth are empirically true or even provable. For example, members of a given culture may believe that a rain god visits their land every spring, and if he approves of their offerings and sacrifices, he will water the seeds they have planted. It is not clear that making offerings to a rain god has anything to do with the production of rain. However, sowing seeds in the spring as part of a general religious rite is a pretty good guarantee that if it rains at all, the crops will grow. Thus myths may have little empirical standing, but they often serve powerful functions for those who believe in them.

Sometimes the functions of myths are so numerous and far-reaching that people cling intensely to the most illusive and simplistic of beliefs. The people of many nations in the history of the world, for example, have believed that their nation was responsible for carrying the message of truth and enlightenment to the rest of the world. In some cases the message has been political, in others religious, and in still others economic. Most often the truly enlightened nations of the world have attempted to impose some combination of political, religious, and economic enlightenment on others. It is hard to demonstrate that these historical efforts to impose a particular culture on the rest of the world have produced many positive effects. The Crusades of the Middle Ages did little for the cause of Christianity either at home or abroad (whatever that cause may have been). The exportation of capitalist models of development to Third World, commodity-based economies, has not succeeded in lifting struggling countries out of poverty and oppression. In fact, most Third World nations have become hopelessly dependent, economically and politically, on a few dominant superpowers. Similarly, the American struggle for freedom and democracy in Latin America and the Pacific Basin has resulted in the growth of totalitarian regimes almost everywhere in the region.

Why do people become so committed to myths that have so little empirical foundation? Why is it that the more elusive the myth, the harder to prove or disprove, the more strongly it is embraced? As suggested, many powerful social beliefs are based less on the capacity to prove or disprove the belief than on the side benefits that follow from the belief. No one could, after all, prove whether or not the German people were superior to anyone else; yet the promotion of that belief based on ancient German mythology enabled a nation to regain its moral purpose, recover from economic disaster, and create a semblance of pride and purpose among its citizens. In a similar fashion, the belief in defending freedom in the world is a hard one to verify or refute. It is possible, after all, that if we did not support "friendly" totalitarian regimes, our enemies would succeed in setting up their own brand of totalitarianism in the same countries. What may matter more than the truth of the belief is whether there are benefits to be gained from *acting as if* the belief were valid. For example, a freedom-loving people may derive from their conviction such advantages as a sense of national purpose and solidarity, a real measure of national security through military strength and conquest, and the economic spoils that flow from the successful "defense of freedom" in foreign wars. When one considers such advantages of believing in noble ideals, it is surprising that any rational person would doubt (at least publicly) a functioning national myth, no matter how dubious its empirical status might be.

The acceptance of myths becomes even more universal when they offer something for everyone. For example, different advantages go to different groups that accept the "defense of world freedom" myth. Cozy ties with Third World governments make for lucrative business climates that benefit the corporate and financial elite. The commitment to military strength makes for big industrial profits and provides jobs for many working people. The idea of doing good in the world gives some people a sense of pride and self-worth. While the same benefits do not go to everyone, many different groups get something out of their acceptance of the myth.

The myth of "a Free Press and a Free People" and its guiding principle of objective reporting provide different but compelling benefits for different groups. However, there is a catch: The groups at the top of the power structure gain the material advantages of power and control, while the groups at the bottom trade real power (since the myth works in reality to limit their political involvement) for psychological reassurances. The irony of this situation is that the broader the support is for the idea of objective journalism, the more firmly established the inequalities of power become. A brief overview of the cases of politicians, journalists, and the public illustrates how different (and even contradictory) the bases of loyalty to a myth can be.

Politicians and the News Myth

The reasons are obvious why political actors display such universal support for the free press, free people myth. The regular proclamation of the myth is both useful and necessary. It is useful to invoke the myth because it is much easier to hide political deception behind a convincing show of support for truth and popular sovereignty. It is necessary for politicians to endorse the news myth because the American public would never tolerate a leader who did not keep up the outward appearances of commitment to democratic ideals. Even if the information agencies of government work overtime to engineer public opinion, the public demands at least the illusion that the government represents their will. The news myth helps create the illusion that the ideals of popular government are still viable.

Politicians affirm the news myth in word and deed. Virtually all leaders and public officials appear locked in battle with reporters at one time or another. As noted in Chapter 2, there is an element of authenticity in the conflict between politicians and reporters because reporters would, if given the rope, hang most politicians. Few news stories are bigger than the fall of a powerful public figure. Therefore, successful political figures must be everwary in their encounters with reporters. Journalists, for their part, must be aggressive in order to maintain the image that they are not easily manipulated. As with politicians, the adversarial posture of journalists has an element of authenticity to it. Even though reporters may be vulnerable to political manipulation, that does not mean that they have to like it.

The more the politician proclaims the public importance of the news myth, the more he or she serves personal interests and the interests of the state on which his or her power depends. It matters little whether politicians are conscious of the contradiction between their public support for the myth and their private efforts to control information. The private political benefits accrue to the true believer in news objectivity as surely as they flow to the cynical politician who takes the news myth in vain.

Journalists and the News Myth

The function of the news myth for the journalist is not power but professional credibility. Without a public commitment to objective reporting, the journalist would lose any claim to professional status or political access. As in the case of the politician, the reporter is provided a ready-made role in the ideal picture of American democracy. Since that role is so easily dramatized with the help of the politician, it would be hard to imagine many reporters not embracing the part. Rather than engage in futile efforts to expose the news game, most reporters who become frustrated with mass media objectivity simply leave the major news organizations to become free-lance writers or reporters for news channels outside the mainstream.

Some journalists, like some politicians, may adopt the cynical attitude of mouthing the news myth while harboring the full knowledge of its emptiness. However, it is reasonable to suppose that many journalists fail to see the contradiction in their pursuit of news objectivity. At some point, the career journalist must accept the fact that reporting what officials say and do is really the highest form of professionalism. The line between objectivity and political distortion in the news is further eroded by adopting the reporting formulas that mark the journalist's craft. Thus it is a small step from the activities of professional, objective journalism to the assumption that these activities really are the keys to revealing the truth about politics. "Telling it like it is" can become equated, however erroneously, with telling the truth. For example, it is hard to imagine any lack of sincerity in these words of Walter Cronkite, the former dean of American newscasters: "... we are all *professional* journalists, dedicated to truth, honesty, to telling it as it is without fear or favour—and . . . there is no politician or bureaucrat who can make that claim."[13] At the time that Cronkite made this statement, he was regarded as the most trusted public figure in the country.[14] Journalists, like politicians, receive their benefits from endorsing the news myth whether or not they are conscious of its contradictions.

The People and the News Myth

But what about the public? What can people gain from deceiving themselves about the quality of information in their lives? In order to answer this perplexing question, we must return to the two pictures of power in America presented earlier in the chapter. The reality of power in America shows the public locked into a weak power position with their choices structured for them and their efforts to respond, politically, filtered through the distorting lens of media formulas. Such a plight would naturally leave most people helpless and wishing for a return to the ideal version of American politics in which press and politicians served the public, rather than the other way around.

Those who wish hard enough for an escape from their political reality may have that wish granted by the magic of the media. Both journalists and politicians continually dramatize the free press, free people myth for the benefit of the public. Most news stories are offered as reports to the people about some choice or problem that faces them. Leaders appeal in the news for popular support and understanding. If people can suspend their concerns about such nagging questions as where media issues come from, how the proposed solutions are chosen, and what the limits of public involvement really are, then it is possible to escape into a world of political drama. In this political fantasy world the people do seem to have choices, leaders do seem to respond to popular input, and the news does appear to monitor the activities of government in the name of the people.

When confronted with a choice between escaping into the satisfying ideals of democracy or facing the unpleasant realities of politics, it is not surprising that many people prefer the former alternative. Nor is it surprising that many people who opt for fantasy politics over more realistic political involvement are able to treat the fantasy world seriously. After all, the public too can call up the myth of a free press and a free people. The public affirmation of the myth is a way of asserting that, in effect, the world of media politics *is* the real world of politics. If people choose to regard media politics as real, then, for all practical purposes, it is real. As long as the news scripts contain suitable roles for the public, and as long as politicians, journalists, and the public endorse the news myth, then it is possible for people to treat the news world seriously.

People may harbor secret doubts about the honesty of government or the authenticity of news, but what good would it do to express those doubts? Who would listen? What could be done? It is unpleasant for people to admit their own helplessness, particularly when comforting social illusions are available. Thus the public, like politicians and journalists, reap certain benefits from endorsing the news myth. It is unfortunate that the "benefits" in the case of the public are so counter to the real interests of the people.

Is There a Solution?

At this point in the book it is tempting to call for sweeping news reforms. If the problems with the news were not caught in the tangle of power and national belief described above, there would be any number of changes that would improve the quality of public information. For example, the journalism profession could advocate the use of interpretive political reporting based on ideology, historical analysis, social theory, or just plain political reasoning. Journalists trained in these interpretive methods could educate the public about politics through the news. The mass media could break out of its enslavement to "two-sided" news and present diverse, provocative political views to the public. The rejection of hidden reporting formulas in favor of grounded interpretive frameworks would give the news audience a basis for developing an active, thinking, reasoning relationship with the political world.

The list of ideal news reforms could go on, but to what end? Who would listen to such recommendations? Who would implement them? As long as press, politicians, and people are locked into their current web of power relations there is little room for sweeping news reforms. Such reforms would entail fundamental changes in American politics, changes that would be resisted at the highest levels of government. Even the public would probably resist these changes since they would view them (with the help of leaders and journalists) as threats to objective reporting and the political order.

Yet the current state of news politics is too serious to tolerate helplessly. If the problems discussed in this book persist, the American people will become ever more isolated from their government and ever more confused about politics. The United States could move toward a sort of "media oligarchy" in which a smaller and smaller number of elites, with increasingly shared interests, dominate the political arena. These media-made elites would, of course, proclaim themselves to be competitive under their familiar guises as liberals and conservatives and Republicans and Democrats. The media, for their part, will continue to legitimize the claims of political competition through the tradition of objective journal-

ism. All the while, the true range of political competition, real deb
and meaningful public participation will grow narrower and narrower.
Something must be done. But what is it?

Simply because the system of news politics will not reform itself
according to our wishes, there is no reason that any individual must fall
into step with it. If a person understands the makeup of mass media news,
he or she is equipped to undertake the individual changes that are necessary to make the news personally useful. Before discussing the nature of
these personal solutions, let's examine the rationale for change at the
individual level.

The idea of individual solutions for a collective problem may not be
entirely satisfying, but the search for personal answers to the news dilemma is by no means an empty exercise. In his masterful novel, *1984*,
George Orwell made a compelling point about political control through
mass communication. The point is that each individual is ultimately responsible for thinking clearly and critically about the political world. People should expect governments to throw up obstacles to independent
thought and actions. People should also expect to encounter social pressure to avoid conflict and controversy, no matter how weak the controversy might be. In the end, however, the individual must reject the
pressures of government and society in favor of reasoned, committed personal views. When people accept the ready-made reality of the media and
government, they abandon their hopes for political freedom and
meaningful control over the world they live in.

Despite the pressures to accept mass communicated political reality,
people have the capacity to resist. The capacity to reject distorted pictures of the world is greatest in a liberal political system like the United
States, which has not yet taken the final turn toward the totalitarian world
of *1984*. American citizens are still free, within limits, to think what they
like and say what they think. Nevertheless, the degree of freedom that
remains in American society is deceptive, in the sense that it leads people
to doubt the need for vigilance and personal courage. It is tempting to
think that there are more important things in life than politics. It is tempting to trust our political affairs to a government that spends a great deal
of energy inviting our trust and presenting political issues as too complex
and technical to warrant our concern.

Although it may be tempting to leave our political thinking to others, it
would be a disaster to do so. The tacit acceptance of the reality presented
in the news is equivalent to abandoning the most basic right on which all
our freedoms depend: the right to formulate independent judgments
about political affairs. Each individual has a personal stake in thinking critically about events in the news and in forming an independent perspective
on the political world.

ntinue to let journalistic formulas and political melo-
views of reality, views that are confirmed only when
back into the distorting lens of the media for support
Lapham observed, the final victory of government
minds of the people can occur only with the coopera-

If the media succeed with their spectacles and grand simplifications, it is because their audiences define happiness as the state of being well and artfully deceived. People like to listen to stories, to believe what they're told, to imagine that the implacable forces of history speak to them with a human voice. Who can bear to live without myths? If people prefer to think that drug addiction causes crime, that may be because they would rather not think that perfectly ordinary people commit crimes, people not too different from themselves, people living in the same neighborhoods and sending their children to the same schools.

The media thus play the part of the courtier reassuring their patrons that the world conforms to the wish of the presiding majority. The media advertise everything and nothing. Yes, say the media, our generals know what they're doing (no, say the media, our generals are fools); the energy crisis was brought down on our innocent heads by the Arabs (the energy crisis is the fault of our profligacy and greed); Vietnam was a crusade (Vietnam was imperialism); homosexuality is a "lifestyle" (homosexuality is a disease); the Kennedys were demigods (the Kennedys were beasts); the state is invincible (the state has lost its nerve); yes, Virginia, there is a reality out there, and not only can it be accurately described, but also it looks just the way you always wanted it to look.[15]

If people are content with these, to borrow Tom Wolfe's phrase, "Vicks-Vapo-Rub" world views, then they also must content themselves with the eventual loss of freedom, value, and meaning. These are heavy prices to pay for the convenience of a ready-made reality full of instant controversy, disappearing problems, and reassurance around every corner. There is an alternative. The reader is equipped at this point to escape from the news prison. Even though the news distorts the political world and inhibits critical thinking, it should be evident by now how it does these things. Armed with this information about how the news works, it should be possible to break the "news code" in virtually any news story and produce a better, more sensible, and more useful interpretation of the reality behind the story.

Discovering the Reality Behind the News

Anyone interested in understanding the reality behind the news should develop a set of guidelines for, first, separating facts from hidden political messages; second, evaluating the remaining facts in terms of reliability or authenticity; and third, developing alternative interpretations for the information that is reliable enough to take seriously.

Separating Fact from Fiction in the News

The first task facing the intelligent news consumer is to learn to detect and then discount the hidden political messages in news stories. The basic message in a news story is most often the result of planned propaganda, formula reporting, or a combination of both. The reader should be able to recognize the characteristics of pseudoevents and other controlled political performances and decipher the political messages they convey. Similarly, it is possible to spot standard reporting formulas and recognize the political slants that they introduce into stories.

Consider an example of how to see through a pseudoevent. When a President announces a "war" on anything, the news consumer should begin looking immediately for signs of a well-planned political drama with a clear political purpose. Such political staging was plainly in evidence when Ronald Reagan declared war on crime after nearly two years in office. He announced his support for a complete package of legislation that would make it tougher for criminals to get away with terrorizing the majority of law-abiding American citizens. The entire performance was designed to rally the support of a fearful, economically troubled citizenry around a strong leader. It was not incidental that the entire performance was staged just two days after Reagan suffered his first major political defeat (Congress overrode his veto of a major federal spending bill). Could the President have had a prepared political diversion waiting in the wings for just such an occasion? What do you think? An attentive news critic should be able to detect the signs of scripted political performances and note how they fit into the political needs and circumstances of the actors who perform them.

The formulas of journalism also must be stripped from the news in order to make it interpretable. When journalists describe a political struggle in terms of standard plots about personal power or party rivalries, the whole point of the issue at stake can be lost. For example, when a prominent conservative senator attempted to add antiabortion and prayer in the schools amendments to a federal spending bill, the news story was built around the personal struggle of a powerful leader with equally determined opponents. The use of this tired plot formula made it hard to see the major questions about the personal use of institutional power and the congressional challenge to judicial authority. The news critic should be able to screen out the formulas in order to bring into focus the neglected aspects of a story.

Evaluating the Facts in the News

Even when political and journalistic formulas have been stripped away from the news, there often remains a hard core of facts and information that lend credence to the issue at stake. While a staged performance or a mechanical news formula can be discounted, it is harder to dismiss seemingly objective evidence. And yet we know that some of the facts in the news are every bit as fictional as the plots that surround them. How do we grapple with the brute data in the news?

As a first step, it is helpful to decide whether the facts really say anything new about the world or whether they are used primarily to lend credibility to a staged political performance. Consider, for example, the role of facts in a presidential crusade against crime. Without citations of rising crime rates, the recurring call for a war on crime might seem entirely transparent. The listing of facts about the crime problem gives the issue a certain measure of credibility even if the facts sound virtually identical each time the issue is revived. Even a critic of the President's motives might find it hard to deny the legitimacy of the issue. Yet why should the same old facts about crime be taken seriously just because the President calls attention to them at a particular time and proclaims that they represent a serious problem? After all, the facts have always been there, and the problem has always been there. If the facts represent a serious and enduring problem, then it makes little sense to take them seriously as support for a short-term "crisis issue." If they are to be useful at all, the standard facts about crime must be taken entirely out of the context of a fragmented, short-lived news story and placed in broader interpretive frameworks. This means, for all practical purposes, that the repetitive facts in familiar news stories are of little value, since the news critic must discount the immediate context of the story in order to make sense of them.

In contrast to the number of seemingly unchanging facts that rise and fall with issues in the news, some facts appear to be both new and pertinent to understanding the specific topic of a news story. These story-specific facts present a different interpretive problem. For example, when the government announced that the land-reform program in El Salvador was successful, based on the best available statistics, what was the public to think? The first thing the news critic should consider about such a case is "who was the source of the information?" If the same agency that is advocating a political position also has control over the gathering and release of supporting information, then the news critic should discount that information. When the State Department cannot show that its information was independently and reliably gathered, then there is no point in regarding the information as "factual" in nature. To the contrary, the news critic should put more stock in competing claims about the facts in question. If "rumors" are reported to the effect that official facts have been inflated, then those rumors should be taken seriously. It is so difficult for even the hint of skepticism about official pronouncements to enter the news that such hints should be weighted heavily by the news critic.

Creating Alternative Interpretations of the News

The detection of story formulas and the evaluation of facts are the preliminary steps in news interpretation. It is also necessary to construct an interpretive framework. This framework must fill in the gaps left by the removal of the story formula and account for the conclusions that have been drawn about the importance and reliability of the facts. As discussed earlier, interpretive frameworks can be derived from historical, theoretical, and ideological perspectives on politics and society. The development of a personal perspective on politics is by no means an inhibition to seeing the world clearly. To the contrary, it is the only way to gain freedom from the bias and distortion of the news.

It is possible to begin developing a personal news perspective simply by learning to recognize patterns of political communication in the news and then deciding how these patterns affect your personal values about freedom, equality, participation, and governmental authority. You are already armed with enough basic ideas from this book to detect the most common political patterns in the news. The next step is to work through your feelings and logical conclusions about various aspects of news politics. For example, you may decide that Presidents always lie about their intentions to enter wars, but some cases seem more justifiable than others. You may condone Franklin Roosevelt's intentions in promising that no American troops would enter World War II while condemning Lyndon Johnson's campaign promise not to commit American fighting forces to Vietnam. After detecting enough historical patterns in news plots, you should be able to: (1) recognize the political gambit involved, (2) avoid being taken in by it, (3) construct a more satisfying personal interpretation for what is going on, and (4) make an evaluation about how acceptable or objectionable the political reality is.

The capacity to recognize (and not be taken in by) the political manipulation in the news is probably reason enough to become a news critic. There is a satisfying feeling that comes from being able to see through deception. If nothing else, successful news interpretation prevents the feelings of frustration, helplessness, and despair that come from finding out, too late, that the government has deceived us once again.

Even more important than defending ourselves against deception is the control offered by news interpretation over the meaning of events in the real world around us. The world can quickly become a meaningless place when we are bombarded by fragmented, distorted, ever-shifting, and disappearing images of it. Yet we need to believe that there is a world of stable meaning around us in order to feel that our lives have purpose and substance. As Joan Didion observed so forcefully:

> We tell ourselves stories in order to live. The princess is caged in the consulate. The man with the candy will lead the children into the sea. The naked woman on the ledge outside the window on the sixteenth floor is a victim of accidie, or the naked woman is an exhibitionist, and it would be "interesting" to know which. We tell ourselves that it makes some difference whether the naked woman is about to commit a mortal sin or is about to register a political protest or is about to be . . . snatched back to the human condition by the fireman in priest's clothing just visible in the window behind her, the one smiling at the telephoto lens. We look for the sermon in the suicide, for the social or moral lesson in the murder of five. We interpret what we see, select the most workable of the multiple choices. We live entirely . . . by the imposition of a narrative line upon disparate images, by the "ideas" with which we have learned to freeze the shifting phantasmagoria which is our actual experience.[16]

If the meaning of our own lives depends so much on how we understand the people and events in the outer world, then it matters a great deal who imposes the interpretations on events in the news. If we accept without question the political messages in news reports, then we have abdicated an important measure of our political freedom. It may be comforting to hear a respected news authority assure us that "that's the way it is," but in the final analysis, we must figure it out for ourselves.

Notes

1. William L. Rivers, "The Social Scientist and the Journalist," in *Watching American Politics*, ed., Dan Nimmo and William Rivers (New York: Longman, 1981), p. 5.
2. For illustrations of these properties of stories, see W. Lance Bennett and Martha S. Feldman, *Reconstructing Reality in the Courtroom* (New Brunswick, N.J.: Rutgers University Press, 1981).
3. David Paletz and Robert Entman, *Media Power Politics* (New York: Free Press, 1981), p. 22.
4. Robert Scholes, "Double Perspective on Hysteria," *Saturday Review* 24 (August 1968): 37.
5. Quoted from John Hohenberg, *Free Press, Free People* (New York: Columbia University Press), p. 124.

6. From Hodding Carter, III, "Time to Trust the Government Again, Right?" *Wall Street Journal*, 28 January 1982, p. 23.

7. Ibid.

8. Ibid.

9. Ibid.

10. Thomas Powers, "But Never Danger Today," *Atlantic*, April 1982, p. 106.

11. Quoted from Howard Simons and Joseph A. Califano, Jr., eds., *The Media and Business* (New York: Vintage Books, 1979), p. xiii.

12. Quoted from Frank Luther Mott, *The News in America* (Cambridge, Mass.: Harvard University Press, 1952), p. 5.

13. Quoted in Marvin Barrett, ed., *The Politics of Broadcasting, 1971–1972* (New York: Crowell, 1973), p. 49.

14. According to an Oliver Quayle poll reported in ibid.

15. Lewis Lapham, "Gilding the News," *Harper's*, July 1981, p. 37.

16. Joan Didion, *The White Album* (New York: Pocket Books, 1979), p. 11.

Index